Revolution in the Theatre:

CONCLUSIONS CONCERNING

the MUNICH ARTISTS' THEATRE

Facade of the Munich Artists' Theatre. From Max Littmann's *Das Münchner Künstlertheater* (Munich: L. Werner, 1908).

Revolution in the Theatre:

CONCLUSIONS CONCERNING

the MUNICH ARTISTS' THEATRE

By Georg Fuchs

CONDENSED AND ADAPTED
FROM THE GERMAN BY

Constance Connor Kuhn

"Rethéâtraliser le théâtre!"

KENNIKAT PRESS
Port Washington, N. Y./London

REVOLUTION IN THE THEATRE

Reissued in 1972 by Kennikat Press by arrangement
Library of Congress Catalog Card No: 73-153214
ISBN 0-8046-1524-1

Manufactured by Taylor Publishing Company Dallas, Texas

This translation is dedicated to the memory of

ALEXANDER M. DRUMMOND

an artist who, as Professor of Speech and Drama at Cornell University, made the theatre a place of wisdom and enchantment, of aspiration and fulfillment; a teacher whose integrity, understanding, and generosity abide in the lives and hearts of his students.

Translator's Preface

OUT of the rubble which in 1945 covered the *Ausstellungs Park* on the outskirts of Munich rose three gaunt portals. These empty entrances, looming against the sky above the gentle knoll of the *Theresenhöhe*, were all that remained of the famous *Künstlertheater* (Artists' Theatre). The building had been designed by the distinguished architect Max Littmann, examples of whose work were to be seen in various parts of Germany at the beginning of the twentieth century. Littmann's theatres were characterized by an austere and elegant simplicity, which was in marked contrast to the rococo and baroque designs commonly appearing in the theatre buildings of that era.

The Artists' Theatre was erected as one of the exhibits in an Exposition of Arts and Sciences held in Munich in 1908. The theatre represented the culmination of a co-operative activity among a group of artists and designers who had been experimenting for some time in the field of theatrical production. The success of the enterprise was immediate. And during the next four decades its techniques and theories were discussed and debated by critics and craftsmen throughout Europe and America. Littmann's architectural drawings, photographs of the theatre, and detailed descriptions of the plays produced are included in many of the most authoritative books on continental stagecraft.[1]

The source of much of this information is contained in *Die Revolution des Theaters* ("Revolution in the Theatre") by Georg Fuchs, written in 1908 and published the following year by Georg Müller of Munich and Leipzig. Although many people were concerned with the undertaking, it was Professor Fuchs who brought about the synthesis of talents and resources that resulted in the Artists' Theatre. He was well known as a dramatic critic and as an essayist in the field of aesthetics. He had also had experience as a playwright[2] and had been closely associated with the artistic life of Munich, while his interest in the civic affairs of Bavaria and his entrée into court society gave him a background which made him peculiarly suited to advance the undertaking that he headed. He served the project not only as an energetic and able executive but also as a competent historian and ardent propagandist.

He had already written two books on theatrical art before the Artists' Theatre was established,[3] and during the time of its inception he published numerous articles describing the techniques of the new stagecraft and expounding its philosophies. *Die Revolution des Theaters* was written upon the successful conclusion of the theatre's first season, and it was well received and widely read. It contained not only a history of the Munich enterprise, but also many of Fuchs's personal beliefs and theories concerning art and culture. Some of this material recapitulates the discussions published in the articles previously mentioned.

If portions of *Die Revolution des Theaters* seem obliquely discursive, it is because they were originally intended to answer arguments raised by certain critics of the period, particularly those whom Fuchs refers to as the "literati."

It has been assumed by many of those who during the past half-century have read about Georg Fuchs and the work of the Munich Artists' Theatre but have not read *Die Revolution des Theaters* that Fuchs's greatest contribution to the art of the theatre was made by publicizing a technical device—i.e., the shallow stage picture that came to be called the relief stage. This, however, was not his chief concern. As he says, it was not his intent "to put a prescription book into the hands of other *régisseurs*."

What he believed to be most important was to revitalize the theatre and to free it from the weight of academic and literary restrictions that had hampered it during the previous decades. In *Die Revolution des Theaters* Fuchs reported that the relief stage technique worked well in Munich, but some other device, he maintained, might be more successful in another locale. And even in Munich, other methods, he felt, were sure to evolve as the theatre grew and developed.

This was still his strongest feeling about the theatre even when I knew him more than twenty years after the publication of *Die Revolution des Theaters*. His watchword, "*Rethéâtraliser le théâtre!*" was more than a slogan,

It signified his conviction that every theatre must fulfill a function in its particular community. He contended that the Artists' Theatre succeeded because it met the specific needs of Munich, but that other technical procedures might be more effective and practical in Paris, or San Francisco, or Montevideo.

The function of the theatre had, he felt, been the same since Aristotle, and the audience was always of first importance. If spectators are to be purged by emotion, one must know what sort of people they are, and what emotions they respond to. Fuchs's impatience with the literati was not because he lacked understanding or appreciation of literary values but because he recognized, as non-theatrical literary people sometimes do not, that the literary quality of a theatrical production is only one among several component parts of a total effect, a complete art form, by means of which catharsis is evoked. The literary script, the technical mounting, and the temperament of the audience are, he believed, interdependent elements and are indispensable to one another.

Professor Fuchs gave me permission to edit and condense his book, and it would seem to be in order here to explain how the following version of *Revolution in the Theatre* came into being.

Several years ago, Alexander M. Drummond, then director of the Cornell University Theatre, asked me to condense and revise for publication the translation of *Die Revolution des Theaters* which I had done as a thesis for my master's degree in theatre arts at Cornell. His desire for a condensation stemmed from the fact that *Die Revolution des Theaters* seemed to him wordy and diffuse, and he instructed me to shorten the manuscript "by at least seventy-five pages."

In order to comply with this request, two procedures were open to me: first, to make cuts in the body of the text and, second, to make cuts within the passages rendered. In the first instance, it seemed advisable to eliminate such passages as appeared repetitious or overwritten. For example, in describing the dancing of Madelèine and the acting of Lili Marberg, Fuchs gives half again as many descriptions of their work as I have included. I chose only such passages as seemed most apt and striking. In the second instance, I have taken into account that in German rhetoric an extended series of adjectives or adverbs may create an effect of force and vitality, whereas in English this device may weaken rather than strengthen the effect. A passage was often more accurately rendered by using one word which, although not a literal translation of any single word in the original sequence, conveyed the overall significance of the series. Similar rhetorical situations arose in regard to expletives and colloquialisms. Slight changes in the wording of transitional passages were necessitated by the shortening of the text. English usage also sanctions shorter sentences and paragraphs. I have tried to make this version, not a literal translation, but an accurate rendition both as to content and as to style.

As to content, it has seemed most important to make manifest Fuchs's line of argument, his primary thesis, and his basic tenets. I have tried also to keep in mind Fuchs's attitude both toward his subject and toward his audience. His attitude toward his subject was one of great urgency and dedication. He was deeply convinced of the importance and universality of his thesis. His audience he saw as consisting first of those who had opposed his project from the start, who were entrenched in the social system of the times and therefore unwilling to countenance change or alteration, and, second, of those who agreed with his beliefs and wished to know more of his techniques. *Die Revolution des Theaters* was intended as an answer to the first of these groups and as an explanation to the second. The theatre, as Fuchs saw it, has no *raison d'être* unless it is vitalizing to an audience. He agreed with George Cram Cook, founder of the Provincetown Players, who once wrote me: "A theatre is a dynamo pouring energy into the nerves of the audience."

As to style, Fuchs's use of the German language reflects his urgency and vitality. It is vivid, lively, persuasive, humorous, ironic, and sometimes sarcastic. These qualities I have been anxious to transmit. It has been said that style is the organization of meaning through form, the interplay of many elements. This is achieved in part by means of rhythm, a quality with which Fuchs deals specifically in the body of his text. Rhythm reflects emotion in the writer and may create emotion in the audience. Whenever possible it should be preserved in the interest of accuracy, for it reflects both the cause and the result of emphasis. In a literal translation the original rhythms are often unavoidably lost by the use of English words with different beats and stresses. It is therefore sometimes permissible to use less literal words in order to reproduce the emotional impact of the original text.

Professor Fuchs told me his story in German, and I have tried to tell it in English as he might have told it if English had been his native language. I might never have made such an attempt if I had not had the privilege of knowing Professor Fuchs and working with him on another project.

This came about in 1930 when I was visiting various European theatres. I knew that the activities of the Artists' Theatre had been brought to a close by World War I and that the building was still standing, though not in use. But I was surprised to find it, after sixteen years, still looking much as it does in the photographs that illustrate the histories of continental stagecraft, its well-known façade set off by the background of the famous beech woods which had been planted by King Ludwig of Bavaria.

A park official showed me through the building, which was in good repair. There was no scenery backstage, but the appointments in the front of the house seemed to be intact. My chief impression was one of extreme cleanliness and order. I remember wondering how it would feel to work in a professional theatre with dressing rooms that had clean windows looking into a park instead of dirty ones opening into an alley. Had it been like this twenty years before when the theatre was at the height of its success? Or had there been dust, and color, and even a little confusion in the excitement of those days? It was hard to imagine. The raffish ghosts that haunt most empty theatres had not lingered here. Perhaps they had been exorcised (*verboten!*) by the spirit of Teutonic *Sauberkeit* that pervaded most German public monuments. I explored the quiet stage, which though described as a "relief stage" was not much shallower than many others I had seen. I thanked the courteous custodian and went to find Professor Fuchs.

In his book, *New Theatres for Old,* Mordecai Gorelik

gives a description of the opening of the Artists' Theatre. "In those days," he writes, "Fuchs was a slim and fair-haired young man of forty, with a humorless expression which was not softened by his pince-nez and a mustache à la William II." The Professor Fuchs I knew in 1930 could not have been more different. He was stocky, bald, and smooth-shaven. His rather long upper lip gave him an air of solemnity that was contradicted by the lively expression of his eyes behind the round lenses of his spectacles. He was living quietly in Munich and engaged in no theatrical enterprises.

I was on my way to Salzburg and Oberammergau, and I was interested in Professor Fuchs's opinion of these famous festivals. His admiration for Max Reinhardt was tremendous. "*Ein magischer Mensch!*" he called him. Salzburg exemplified to Fuchs the festival spirit which he had always considered an indispensable milieu for the sort of theatrical accomplishment he himself found most satisfying. The romantic beauty of the environment, the elegance and opulence with which Reinhardt's productions were staged, the glamour of his international audiences—all appealed to Fuchs. He was impatient with those critics who found the luxuriant profusion of Reinhardt's effects too rich for their taste. He would point out with emphasis Reinhardt's meticulous attention to detail. "Everything you see and everything you hear is calculated," he would say. "The voices that call to Everyman from the towers of the cathedral are orchestrated. They must strike a certain musical note because that sound—and no other—can create the emotional response that is necessary at that moment. It is quite true that many of Reinhardt's productions have a quality of oriental splendor. They are often voluptuous [*üppig*]. But the exuberance is not haphazard. It bears no relation to realism. It is highly selective."

His praise of Oberammergau was more restrained. "You must see it," he said. "It has historical significance and parts of it are very impressive. Who could fail to be moved by the Crucifixion? There are some fine actors —Judas in particular. As for the text, its literary quality is mediocre. It still smacks of the pedantic ministrations of the village schoolmaster who revised it. The production is no longer genuine [*echt*]. It has come a long way from the *Bauernfest* that Devrient admired. The very piety of the peasants was their undoing. In their desire to put at the service of God all that was best and finest, they fell prey to the salesmen of theatrical devices who swarmed down from Munich and Berlin to offer them 'the very latest in stage scenery and equipment.' They began to doubt their own good taste. The result is a hodgepodge. God gave them their scenery! No outdoor play could have a better background than the Bavarian Alps. Why build a false temple in front of the mountains?—The village itself is charming. You will find it all neat and clean and newly painted. If the atmosphere is rather Thomas Cook and Son—well, one can't have everything!"

After my return from Oberammergau we talked of other, less famous, religious plays performed in the peasant villages near Munich. One of these is described in the first chapter of *Die Revolution des Theaters.* (The village of Dachau had no significance in those days. Half a century later it is startling and macabre to find this locale described as the scene of a peasant Manger play distinguished for its sincerity and great simplicity)

In the course of our conversations Professor Fuchs told me that he himself had once written a *Passionspiel.* He was moved to the undertaking by the situation in which he found himself at the outbreak of the war. Because of a heart ailment he was not drafted, but the Artists' Theatre was closed and he found no scope for his dramatic activities. As an entrepreneur his resources were drastically curtailed. The ranks of Munich artists were depleted; financial backing was difficult to come by; a rigid censorship imposed restrictions he found impossible to accept. He felt himself out of tune with the times and apprehensive of the future. As a relief for his own frustrations as well as an outlet for his creative energies, he turned to dramaturgy. Choosing a supremely exalted theme, he wrote a *Passionspiel*—not in imitation of any of the religious peasant festivals and not as a reconstruction of a medieval miracle play, but as a drama designed to be produced in a modern theatre, to be performed in all reverence by professional actors, and to be staged in such a way as to make use of the most advanced and improved stage devices. When, on completion of the play, he was investigating the possibilities for its presentation, he was encouraged by certain of his monarchist connections to approach court circles in Berlin. Here the manuscript found a ready welcome, and rather to his surprise Fuchs found his way made easy. The Kaiser, well known for his protestations of conventional piety, approved the project as an aid to the morale of his troubled subjects and gave it his support and assistance. Actors, scene designers, and technicians were recalled from the trenches, and Fuchs found the theatrical resources of the Reich placed at his disposal.

Only one of his desires was denied him. As the play had taken shape in his mind, he had said to himself, "This would be something for Reinhardt!" He had been instrumental in bringing Max Reinhardt to Munich in the early days of the great director's career. He felt that his *Passionspiel* would afford Reinhardt an ideal vehicle for his talents and a theme with which he was sympathetic. (The success of Reinhardt's subsequent production of *The Miracle* indicated the truth of these suppositions.) Fuchs therefore suggested that Reinhardt be invited to direct the *Passionspiel.* The proposal was immediately rejected. Professor Reinhardt, he learned, was not *persona grata* at Potsdam. The prejudice that Fuchs suspected lay back of the veto was never admitted. The explanation given was that the Emperor refused to endorse Reinhardt because of Reinhardt's early connection with Otto Brahm, whose production of Gerhart Hauptmann's *The Weavers* the Kaiser had chosen to label "dangerous socialistic propaganda." At the time of that production Reinhardt had been a young and inconspicuous actor in Brahm's theatre and had not even appeared in the offending play. No appeal, however, was possible and the *Passionspiel* was staged by another director. It was an outstanding success in Berlin and toured the German Reich. It was translated into Hungarian and opened in Budapest, where it also attracted large audiences.

Professor Fuchs brought me a copy of the play, which I examined with interest. "Why don't you translate it?" he suggested. "I know that Professor Reinhardt would be interested to produce it in England—or possibly in America. We've had some correspondence about it." I admitted that I'd like to try it. "It should not be too difficult," he said, "if you keep as close to the King James Bible as I have done to the Luther version."

I found Professor Fuchs to be an interesting companion. He was proud of the theatre as a profession and of the fact that Shakespeare, Molière, and Goethe were concerned not only with writing plays but with producing them. "The literati," he used to say, "find it embarrassing that so much of the world's best literature was written for the theatre. They treat the drama like a fallen woman who should be rescued from a *déclassé* environment. It's amusing to watch them tiptoeing through the fertile fields of the theatre, stooping to pluck the pure blossoms of literature out of the rich, warm earth that has nourished them. And this ridiculous gesture they make without soiling a finger! They collect little, literary nosegays (*Sträusschen*), which they sniff at and swoon over like adolescents. They have no real love of the theatre but only infantile crushes (*Schwärmerie*). And these they would prefer to indulge in solitude."

I ventured a query: "What about those who in all honesty say that in their imaginations they can create a more satisfying setting for a play than even the most perfect production can furnish?"

"That," he replied with amusement, "is not creation. It's self-delusion. It is as though one said, 'I take less pleasure in hearing a fine orchestra perform the works of Beethoven than I do in playing the Ninth Symphony on a penny whistle.' Such whistling is not creative. It's a waste of breath. It does not even keep up the courage. It only inflates the ego. One cannot enjoy the full flavor of a theatrical experience except as part of an audience.

No sane person wants to attend a theatrical production in solitary state. Few people have had the opportunity to do so—except Ludwig of Bavaria. And he, they say, was mad."

While I busied myself with a translation of the *Passionspiel*, Professor Fuchs came frequently to inspect my efforts and to give advice. He also helped me to become acquainted with Munich. His pride in the city was not only in the broad avenues and palatial buildings which proclaimed it a *Hauptstadt* and a Royal Residence but also in certain humbler, less conspicuous sections, which gave him particular pleasure. And he felt that it was not sufficient for a visitor to see the art galleries and inspect the points of historical interest. "I shall show you a stage-set for *Die Meistersinger*," he would say, "some very old houses leaning toward each other across a narrow street. We must be there in the early afternoon when the sun shines between the gables. Then they look immensely tall!" Later, standing in the narrow *Gasse* peering up at a patch of sky, he pointed out, "It's all a matter of proportion. In New York your streets are wider, but I imagine that your skyscrapers [*Wolkenkratzer*] give much the same effect." In the distance a youth in a faded blue shirt leaned against a yellow wall, and Professor Fuchs remarked, "It's very obliging of the 'supers' to wear such harmonious colors."

We went for walks in the English Gardens, where the swans floated on the lake beside the Chinese Tower. I visited the *Oktoberfest* and enjoyed the *Bratwürste* and the merry-go-rounds. "All *that*," he said with approval, "is still *echt!*"

As time for the German elections approached, political

slogans and posters began to appear on the walls of Munich. The vulgar doggerel and scurrilous cartoons were more incendiary than anything I had ever seen in America. Many of them puzzled me. There were dozens of different parties. It was very confusing. "Who," I inquired, "is this Adolf Hitler?" "A rabble-rouser," Fuchs replied. "Do you think I should go to hear him?" I asked. "I don't know why you should," he said. "He's of no consequence.—But you must be sure to attend the production of Shaw's *Saint Joan* at the little theatre in Schwabing. It's presented by a company of boys from Harrow and they give a delightful performance."

We talked of a variety of subjects. Of Shakespeare's death mask, of witchcraft in the Alpine villages, of mad King Ludwig, and of the lost continent of Mu. But when I asked him to explain the German political parties to me, he merely shrugged. When I suggested that he might not be much interested in politics, he said, "I have been [*Ich war einmal*]," and then added, "Perhaps you don't know where I was when you were first reading my book about the *Künstlertheater*." "No," I said, "where were you?" "In prison," he replied, and went on to tell me of certain events in Bavaria which followed World War I.

Fuchs had always been an ardent royalist. He had been instrumental in obtaining the support of the House of Wittelsbach for the Artists' Theatre, which opened under the patronage of Prince Rupprecht. After the defeat of Germany Fuchs saw Munich, as he described it, "overrun by a Communistic carpetbag government from Berlin." In order to stem the tide of what he felt to be a wave of violence and misrule, he joined in a conspiracy to set up an independent royalist government in Bavaria. He was delegated to solicit funds in France, a mission which he was able to accomplish by representing his operations as activities in behalf of the artistic and nonpolitical enterprises with which he had always been identified. The plot was betrayed from within, and Professor Fuchs and two other conspirators, both better known as artists than as politicians, were indicted. Of these fellow prisoners Fuchs reported that "one of them committed suicide in prison and the other was 'taken for a ride' in the best Chicago fashion." Fuchs was brought to trial and sentenced to twelve years in the penitentiary. The highly placed royalists who had headed the plot were never indicted. At the time of his incarceration Fuchs was seriously ill. He was convinced that, because of the precarious state of his health, his judges believed the imposition of a twelve-year sentence was tantamount to life imprisonment.

The first months of his sentence were spent in solitary confinement, an experience which he later avowed results for most human beings either in a complete collapse or in an unprecedented strengthening of the individual's mental and emotional fiber. During his imprisonment he found his jailers as lenient as was possible under the circumstances, a fact which he believed was accounted for by their secret sympathies with the objectives which had landed him in prison. They allowed him to have writing materials, and he occupied himself with various literary projects, one of which was an account of his incarceration, with recommendations for prison reform.[4]

When he had served six years of his sentence, he was released under an edict whereby, on Hindenburg's eightieth birthday, all political prisoners of the Reich were pardoned. Upon his return to his family, he found his wife an invalid. The inflation which followed the war had decimated their financial resources. His daughter had obtained a position with a law firm specializing as tax experts, and her earnings barely sufficed for their support when augmented by the returns her father received from such books and articles as he was able to publish. These were mainly of a sociological and philosophical nature.

When the English version of the *Passionspiel* was completed, I went to Berlin with an introduction from Professor Fuchs to Professor Reinhardt. At that time there were four successful theatres running in Berlin under Reinhardt's management. He spoke with appreciation of the *Passionspiel.* "I'd like very much to do an English version of the play," he said, "but preferably in America. I have been seriously considering another American tour. It may be very important to me. When you return to New York I should like you to see Rudolf Kommer, who is my representative there."

When I returned to New York, Mr. Kommer came to see me. "I know Georg Fuchs's *Passionspiel,*" he said, "and I appreciate Professor Reinhardt's interest in producing it. It would require a stupendous mounting; and where, in these depression days, would one get financial backing for it? I think it likely that Professor Reinhardt will soon come to America. Probably to Hollywood. But I'm afraid the *Passionspiel* is not the sort of play the motion picture people have in mind for him."

During the next decade I had occasional communications from Professor Fuchs. His references to world affairs were guarded, but they indicated that he was deeply distressed and sorely beset. "I have managed to explain my ancestry," he wrote me in the late thirties. "That is a matter of record. But my friends and associates are matters of record too. They are apparently not so acceptable to my inquisitors."

I feared that during the bombing of Munich Professor Fuchs might have been killed. Or that, since I knew he must be nearly eighty, he might have died—perhaps as a result of the hardships and privations which always afflict the elderly in time of war. But with the first communications delivered by the Red Cross after the cessation of hostilities, I received a message from him. He was still in Munich, living in a home for the aged. "I am better off than many people," he wrote. "The most painful thing about my situation is that the subsistence diet leaves one too weak for any sustained creative effort. But I manage to write a little. It is heartening to know that the ideas I expounded over a generation ago are still of interest." My last news of him came on a package returned to me in 1949, stamped with the single word—*Gestorben.*

CONSTANCE CONNOR KUHN

Poughkeepsie, New York
August, 1958

Preface

THE Munich Artists' Theatre was born of the spirit of formalization in German art, a spirit which reached its most perfect technical development in the artistic life of Munich. It was my close association with the artistic circles of Munich which made it possible for me to become the founder of the Artists' Theatre. Whatever I myself have created in an artistic or literary way has been nurtured by the atmosphere in which I have lived. And if my studies of the past decade have provided me with experience which has proved useful as a foundation for the Artists' Theatre, it is because I have shared a common background with those theatre artists whose work has contributed to the success of our project.

It is not my intention here to give a critical or even a historical summation of our enterprise. The time for this has not yet come. If the Artists' Theatre were to attempt to present a series of final solutions to the problems of stage production, we who are most closely concerned would know better than anyone else how many important and difficult tasks still remain to be accomplished. Nor am I attempting to set forth a new system of aesthetics. I shall deal only with certain *fundamental* problems, such as the place of the theatre in our modern culture.

The reproduction of pictures showing scenes from the Artists' Theatre—to be used as illustrations—has been considered inadvisable. Such reproductions would give entirely false impressions and inevitably lead to erroneous conclusions. Photographic experiments were conducted in the Artists' Theatre with the most advanced apparatus. The results, without exception, proved unsatisfactory. Drama is unhampered movement. The photographic plate preserves only a moment of repose and thus by its very nature contradicts one of the basic laws of drama. By the same token, it would be a mistake to reproduce here the working drawings which the artists made for various scenes and productions. These are merely "pictures." The Artists' Theatre did not make use of "living pictures," but rather of a succession of dramatic scenes. These artists' sketches were never used as "stills" are used in making moving pictures. The essentially dramatic transformation of ideas into visual form cannot, unfortunately, be shown by illustrations. If one made the attempt, in an effort to put a sort of prescription book into the hands of theatrical practitioners, the results would be unfortunate.

Certain literary men in Germany, especially certain playwrights, have been bitterly hostile to the Artists' Theatre and to its cultural aims. The reason for this, when it can be laid to specific causes, will be explained in the present volume. This explanation is not given out of any desire to meet enmity with enmity or to attribute to personal animosity any greater importance than it has. On the contrary, I hope that a candid discussion may induce the literary men of Germany—hiding behind barriers of an aesthetic trade-unionism—to abandon a position which has become untenable.

My productions have, I admit, been violently attacked, even after their presentation at the Artists' Theatre had proved them to be artistically, mechanically, and financially successful. I am well aware that the acceptance or denial of the position I claim for the theatre is not primarily a matter of aesthetics but a question of philosophy. Whenever one contemplates radical changes in taste, one has to discard those past productions which are still on hand—in this instance, whole libraries of dramatic literature. That those who thus feel themselves threatened should put up a relentless opposition, is quite understandable. It might, however, be well for them to remember that when the corresponding change in taste took place in the field of so-called applied art, those persons came off best in a business way who, although they may have publicly protested against "the revolution," yet quietly made alliance with the victorious forces of the "new movement" and thereby advanced themselves decades beyond their rivals.

It has been necessary in the following exposition to discuss the general cultural changes and the new standards growing out of these changes as they appear in the theatre, the drama, and the art of acting. I hope to show that our cultural renaissance must ultimately lead to a revolution in the art of the theatre, a revolution which all the other arts have fought triumphantly; which has freed them from the yoke of literature, and from all other ties which are not a legitimate part of their particular artistic entity. "*Rethéâtraliser le théâtre!*" With this motto I launch my discussion.

GEORG FUCHS

Munich
October 15, 1908

Contents

Illustrations

All the illustrations have been reproduced from Max Littmann's book, *Das Münchner Künstlertheater* (Munich: L. Werner, 1908), with English translations for the German legends on the figures.

Revolution in the Theatre:

CONCLUSIONS CONCERNING *the* MUNICH ARTISTS' THEATRE

I

The Theatre and Culture

WHY do we go to the theatre? If we answer this question with candor, we shall have to admit that we go to the theatre for excitement and for entertainment. In fact, we attend a play in much the same spirit in which our ancestors assembled to witness a witch trial or to watch a hanging. Moreover, we prefer to enjoy such excitements in the company of others. But, above all, we want to be amused. We are resentful whenever we are bored.

The author of the play may have achieved many noteworthy objectives. He may have expounded the most serious subjects—exploring the heights of human experience, plumbing the depths of the human soul. But if in so doing he has bored us, we do not forgive him.

One evening recently I passed a theatre; one of my friends came hurrying down the steps of the imposing entrance. It was, I suspect, between the second and third acts. (Nowadays most of us dash from the playhouse before the performance is over because we have usually been bored with it from the beginning!) My friend, being a man of taste, was indignant.

"I admit," said he, "that I wanted entertainment and that I hoped to find it in the theatre on a more intellectual plane than at the circus. I expected to enjoy myself in more varied company than at my club, with more sensitivity than at a ball, and with more wisdom and taste than in any of these places. But I wish I could tell you what a miserable time I have had! And all the while I felt I should assume an air of great enjoyment—because the author of this piece is one of our most famous men of letters. But let me tell you what he did to me!

"First, he introduced me into a company of ill-bred people; then he forced me to witness the mawkish behavior of sentimental weaklings and to listen to the vulgar speech of common characters. And after that he exhorted me to champion the diseased, the decrepit, and the oppressed, until, in the end, I myself felt diseased, decrepit, and oppressed.

"If I had wished to acquaint myself with common degradation, I might better have gone to a brothel. Or if I was supposed to develop my sociological impulses and my powers of observation, I should have fared better in a factory, a hospital, a prison, or a madhouse. What is the purpose of such a performance? Is it supposed to make me acknowledge my sins, repent, and do penance? Very well! But then I should prefer to go to church. Am I supposed to perceive the beauty of common things, the tragedy of the average man? Splendid! But in that case I shall stay at home.

"It's not that I am trying to escape reality. Nor do

I recommend that the stage be censored because of bourgeois notions of propriety. All I ask of the theatre is that it move me deeply. To experience deep and powerful emotion is what I go there for. But if what is beautiful and noble is to move me, it should be shown me accurately. If the mean and ugly are to grip me, they too should be presented with ruthless exactitude, although I have found, only too often, that these modern authors depict the exceptional in as vulgar a fashion as they present vulgarity itself!

"Tonight, wishing to be in harmony with the scene around me, I dressed myself in my best. The charming ladies about me had chosen their costumes with care. The building was like a palace, ablaze with lights, adorned with bronze and marble. And for what? This magnificent setting, all these elaborate preliminaries,[1] ending only in irritation and in ennui. How utterly absurd! In the future I shall side with those who shun the theatre as a pernicious place."

Such an analysis of the theatre is not profound, but it may help us to consider just what needs and desires in the life of modern man the theatre is designed to satisfy. I suspect that certain theories of aesthetics and of style have grown out of the manner in which these needs are met.

2

There is a strange intoxication which overcomes us when, as part of a crowd, we feel ourselves emotionally stirred. Scientific investigation may perhaps determine from what distant ancestors we inherit the proclivity for such intoxication. But whether it springs from primitive orgies or from religious cults, this is certain: there is an emotion which runs through each of us when, as part of a crowd, we find ourselves united in an overwhelming passion.

This is the same compulsion which in one place draws peasants into the frenzy of a fair and, in another, inflames a city populace to mob violence or to revolution. It is this force which in the united tread of a battalion sweeps even a weakling on to deeds of glory.

In modern times we seldom have the opportunity to take part in pageantry,[2] to be swept into the tumult of unbridled festivals, or, cudgel in hand, to storm the stronghold of injustice. Therefore we seek new forms—sometimes simple, sometimes more complex—by which we may savor the old enchantment. Dressed in our best apparel we assemble in fine buildings. We are there to see and to be seen. We stream through crowded halls and feast our senses upon splendor, diversity, sounds, moods, lights—upon stray perfumes and the heat of the mob.

This is our strongest desire, even today. As an afterthought we may perhaps be interested in art. Though in the end we may find that art is really nothing more than a systematic and well-organized technique for the satisfaction of that atavistic urge—the primitive greed for intensification of life.

All these things are part of a single experience—the converging multitude, the common mood, the shared desire, the form in which art manifests itself, the building which contains it, where it is assembled and arranged, where each element becomes part of the entire spectacle.

But let us beware of reformers, most of them literary men, who would take drama out of the theatre, who recommend that we give ourselves solely to "Literature," to literature which is unrelated to life and to its pleasures.[3] They advocate an art which did not spring inevitably from life itself and concerning which they feel anxiety lest it fail to hold its own against the forces of life. So they would dissipate the crowd, separate each man from his fellows, and in so doing, lose entirely the potent force, the primitive enchantment, which is the soul and essence of drama.

3

Return to the theatre! Here is a building ablaze with light. It fills with people, with many sorts of people—all expectant. They greet each other, they chat, they joke, they smile at one another, they look about them. Here is a beautiful woman, there a distinguished man. Here the shimmer of glossy curls, there the flash of jewels. The royal and the great, familiar friends and mysterious strangers, the heroes and heroines of intrigues and adventures, enigmatic personages, provocative coquettes—the frivolous, joyous, bedizened "mob," the world, the whole, great, beautiful world!

And we are a part of it all! We catch our neighbors' glances, envious and admiring, mocking and hostile. People are talking of us too, there perhaps with esteem, here certainly with malice. The tempo quickens, the volume rises. There is a humming, a roar like the waves of the sea. We are caught up in a mood of heightened expectation. Something, we know, is about to happen. There is a chime of bells,[4] a musical chord, a shift of light, a pre-emptory voice. Something *is* happening. Let us see. Let us hear.

One has much the same feeling when, in a drawing-room, someone from a group goes to the piano and strikes a chord, or when, at a fair, as people crowd through the midway, a clown springs upon a platform and begins to sing and caper. Let us see. Let us hear.

What do we see? What do we hear? Perhaps—who knows?—quite by accident, it may be art. Surely, not by accident, we say. It must be by intention. For being neither peasants nor barbarians, nothing inartistic can possibly please us. (This naïve assertion may indeed be the basis for an entire theory of aesthetics.) We do not like to think that art has evolved merely as a climax for our social pleasure, after the refinement of our culture would no longer allow us to enjoy ourselves in cruder ways.

4

We attend the theatre for "pleasure." But who are "we"? As we ask ourselves this question we begin to realize what extremely intricate cultural and social problems confront us when we seriously investigate the basic principles of stagecraft. The problem of the stage becomes for us the problem of the whole of modern society. Every age and every society has the theatre of which it is worthy; and no one, not even the most absolute dictator, not even the most influential artist, can force another on it.

Formerly, the literary theorists separated stage and auditorium. There, beauty was to be. And here, something else—something which was of no account to them. They called it "the public" and ignored it as a shadowy neuter entity. But, if we accept this theory, we must throw into the discard the discoveries of the past hundred years. We shall have to admit that in the field of aesthetics our practice has lagged a century behind our knowledge. For whatever one may say, this much is certain: the public is always right. All the lectures of the critics, all the curses of the literati, all the ridicule of the satirists, all the theories of the reformers have accomplished nothing save to cultivate in the public mind a distrust of literary criticism as it applies to the theatre.

And so the gulf which divided the "loftier" (that is, the "literary") stage from the auditorium became deeper and wider and finally unbridgeable. Both sides forgot they were originally one. Both lost their grasp on the underlying principles of their existence. Audiences no longer admitted the compulsion which brought them into the playhouse; they did not recognize the feeble reflex they experienced there as a remnant of the overwhelming transport that once drove them into the temple of the muses. In the end they actually believed they came to the theatre only for "culture." And so the modern stage was founded on the theoretical need of the masses for cultivation and refinement. People no longer really understood what the theatre was all about.

For us, the excitement, the exaltation of the watching crowd, is the essential thing. It is from this intoxication that the performance springs. It is out of this experience that art is evolved as soon as the cultural development of the audience demands it. In the theatre, art can fulfill its purpose—become an independent and specifically theatrical art—only when it engenders something of this primitive excitement and throws it back again into the audience. The more this excitement is intensified, the more specifically theatrical this art will be. What is called the "effectiveness" of the drama depends upon this circumstance. This is the reason that those who wish to assess the drama solely according to standards of artistic skill, of wit, or of cleverness, find it so difficult to form a judgment. Art, wit, and cleverness are effective only in a secondary way. It is the emotional excitement which is always most important.

The most naïve song, the most witless actor, the most clumsy piece may be "effective" if in some way they send this breath of enchantment out across the crowd. Even the obscurities of poetic drama, which to any individual in the audience may, in their profoundest meaning, be quite incomprehensible, will nevertheless be understood if in some mysterious way they can arouse this primitive excitement. Even today it is the desire for this intoxication of the spirit which drives us into the theatre. Even our high-brow Philistines cannot conceal behind an accumulation of specious poses the degree to which this impulse moves them. He who doubts the truth of this has never seen the glowing eyes of the women when Egmont goes rejoicing to his death, or noted how the dullest burgher lifts his head in triumph when Mark Antony speaks to the Romans.

When this element is lacking, the highest achievements in literature as well as in art count for nothing. That everything depends on this emotion is proved by the fact that even the most hackneyed theme is still effective if it brings about something of this exaltation.

In the world of art we are emerging from a period of suspended animation. The rise of machine civilization destroyed our ancient culture and threatened to change the earth into a heap of coal dust. The integrity of races disappeared in the rush of uprooted peoples to the larger cities. Old forms gave way, new ones did not appear. But the sight of life without form was unendurable. Man hastened to cover the formlessness of things. And after the manner of all pioneers, men clung to shabby imitations of the forms in which the noblest races of antiquity had grasped the meaning of life and had expressed it.

Now a new society is developing, a society made up of members of the younger generation too vital to be crushed by a machine civilization. They have made themselves masters of the machines and are determined to use them as a means of expression for their creative energy, determined to force them into some sort of form. Just as our forefathers created their cultural life out of the stylized elements of their simple handicrafts, so shall we too create a culture peculiarly our own through a similar domination of our more complicated machine age.

This movement has only just begun, but already it has developed tremendous proportions. It represents a society in sharp contrast to the chaotic world of the "general public" with its parvenu pseudo culture. The men and women of this group are among the most gifted, the most thoughtful, the most important in Europe. In them lies the hope of the future. Everything they build stands firm, because it stands on a sound foundation. These people are widely scattered, and all of them are not yet conscious of their relationship to one another. A center for their activity has been lacking. To supply this center, this focus for their energies, has been our problem. Our own particular solution lies in the stage of the future.

Let me repeat: Every society has the theatre of which

it is worthy, and no one can force another on it. The general public has such a theatre. Let us leave it to them. Let us not demand of the conventional theatre things which the general public does not want and never will. We are not required to reform what exists. Our obligation is toward new creation, the creation of a theatre for those who do not yet have one worthy of them.

5

In the past the culture of Germany was predominantly literary in spirit. Recently this type of culture has been giving way to more universal forms, the driving force of which is more artistic than critical or literary in its origin.

Leaders in the field of literature greeted the establishment of the Artists' Theatre with a certain nervous anxiety which was in itself significant. They prophesied that the egotism of the workers in the plastic arts would smother the drama and the actors with symbolism and with unsuitable decoration. The opposite was true. With an unselfishness born of a truly creative spirit, the artists put themselves entirely at the service of the drama and of the actors.

It was natural that at first the decorative elements in the Artists' Theatre attracted more attention from the critics and from the public than ever before, since during the first performances the efforts at reform were directed toward this particular field. But, as soon as the new methods of staging become familiar, they may be expected to attract no more attention than their use in the drama justifies. At any rate, they will be less obtrusive than was the old-fashioned stage equipment with its superfluity of elaborate detail. Our whole endeavor is to obtain the best results by the simplest means. In the Artists' Theatre, as in applied art generally, artistic skills are substituted for technical ones. And these artistic skills call for correspondingly more precise technical tools.

The mechanical and artistic procedures which the theatre formerly used were the most backward of techniques. Consider even the architecture and the decoration of the playhouses. Any barracks, any school, even any jail, is constructed with more art and dignity than are the ostentatious theatre buildings of the past four decades.[5]

And the scenery! Such a senseless waste of technical resources is today insupportable. In our modern living we take technical proficiency for granted. Even our newspapers educate the most unworldly of us to an understanding of the principles of increased production. We have become so insistent on good service that we are angry if earlier devices are not replaced by newer, simpler, more economical inventions. If we demand so much of locomotives, telephones, automobiles, bicycles, and fountain pens, if we at once desert in contempt any doctor or dentist who does not use the most efficient instruments and anesthetics—those that give the best results with the least effort—it is easy to see why we also demand the same efficiency in the theatre.

Let us suppose, for example, that the scenic apparatus for *The Twilight of the Gods* breaks down at every performance, even though the most elaborate machinery is in use. Since the apparatus consistently gives trouble, it becomes obvious that it is constructed on a false principle. A locomotive which constantly ran off the rails would soon be scrapped. Only in the theatre would one put up, in patient impotence, with such arrangements. If, on the other hand, the principles of the theatre were applied to the technicalities of transportation, they would not lead to the use of steam and electricity to accommodate an increase in travel. Theatrical principles applied to transportation would result in a plan whereby one would lash together a hundred hansom cabs and hackney coaches, hitch to them a few dozen ancient nags, and for decoration light the whole contraption with jack-o'-lanterns. The old stage technique made use of modern inventions only in secondary matters. In the main, it neglected to harness the motive power which alone can satisfy the demands of taste, the mastery of design.

Moreover, the very existence of a public with a more exacting, a more artistic and cultivated taste was questioned. Why build a theatre for a handful of aesthetes, artists, and snobs? Even though they might accede to the principles involved, such an enterprise seemed, especially to certain literary people, to be a quixotic venture. Continually immersed in books, and oblivious to the realities of the life around them, the literati overlooked the fact that the waves of a cultural renaissance, engendered by engineering and applied art, had already swept over the upper strata of all circles of society, all callings, and all classes. It is no longer only the "artistic" or "literary" person who takes part in our modern cultural development. It is no longer true that others are shut out. Now the highest types of individuals from all classes make common cause with us in matters of culture. There are monarchs and ministers, scholars and burgomasters, clerics and magistrates, capitalists and laborers, technicians and military men, journalists and statesmen, artisans and landowners, physicians and philosophers, and their taste is the same as that of the artists whose pictures they admire and whose ideas of art they accept.

The time has passed when the author of a little volume of strange verses was unquestionably more esteemed as a cultural influence than the builder of a bridge or the organizer of a world-wide business enterprise. The audience for the Artists' Theatre was at hand before the theatre itself was established. All that was necessary was that this audience be brought together in one place, for its members were scattered throughout the length and breadth of German cultural life.

Judging by the number of visitors to the Artists' Theatre, this new public runs into tens of thousands. And it includes the most advanced, the most influential, the most distinguished members of very rank and of every calling. There was not a performance in the Artists' Theatre at which one did not meet men who embodied the highest ideals of their particular professions. And all of them said, "Here, at last, we have a theatre which is *ours!*" By this they did not mean the one particular theatre, for in it there was much that was imperfect. They meant rather the principles which it exemplified.

We have need of a new theatre, not because the conventional theatre does not satisfy the public, but because alongside this general public, which is still quite satisfied, there has arisen another public with new standards.

Formerly most of us went to the theatre only under compulsion. We said, "The theatre is for the general public." And in so saying we removed ourselves from those who still found satisfaction there—although there were already few enough of these! Only high-school boys and boarding-school girls and "misunderstood" wives came away fully satisfied from the conventional temple of the muses. The mature man, engaged in the keen struggle of modern enterprise, stood aloof from the theatre with ill-concealed contempt. He did not go there to find fulfillment but forgetfulness, and only when no better means of diversion were at hand. Very few people with a mature outlook on life took the theatre seriously.

6

The question has been raised as to whether the theatre can influence the moral and aesthetic development of personality and, if so, in what way. Such theorizing shows that the theatre had once more become a vital problem. For, ultimately, such speculation ends with the query: Has the theatre any value in itself? Or is the stage in modern times only a place of sensationalism and frivolity? Is it perhaps a tribunal for the noisy discussion of current problems,[6] or an amusement place of questionable character? At any rate, the theatre has been dismissed as of doubtful worth in the modern scale of values. The personalities who have been of most decisive influence in developing these values—Schopenhauer, Taine, Nietzsche—all have treated the stage as a cultural influence of dubious worth. Indeed, in its conventional form they definitely rejected it. And all the modern masters of plastic art have done the same—Feuerbach and Leibl, Böcklin, and all the younger men.

If, however, one probes farther into the consciousness of the leading artists and philosophers of our time, one finds that this harsh disinclination is directed only against the conventional stage of the present. They seem to judge the theatre so severely only because they feel so strongly that immense cultural achievements are possible in the theatre. The contrast between this possibility and the actuality—*this* is the source of their dissatisfaction. This contrast alienated not only those whom the younger generation looks upon as leaders. It oppressed us all. Everyone has been disillusioned by his own experience. To every child his first acquaintance with the theatre is a great event. It is of no consequence what he sees—some crude show given in a barn, a children's play, a silly pantomime, a classic tragedy, a music drama by Wagner—it makes no difference. For the child, it is a tremendous experience. It would be difficult to find a person, no matter how old, who does not recall it exactly. Many have forgotten the faces of their parents, but they can still ape the gestures of the comic actors who delighted them on this occasion. We know, not only from the testimony of distinguished men and women but from our own experience, what exaltation overcomes a child on his first visit to the theatre. It is an experience of great intensity and affects his entire being, transporting his senses, informing his imagination, rejoicing his soul. The impressions which rush in upon him during this heightened transport of the spirit, this intoxication of the senses, this welling up of the life force within him is undoubtedly portentous if not decisive in his whole development.

In older civilizations, this knowledge was understood and used. Goethe said to Eckermann,

A great dramatic poet, if he is productive and at the same time possessed of a strong and noble mind, can so create that the soul of his pieces becomes the soul of the people. I have thought that this would be something well worth the effort. Corneille exerted an influence capable of exalting the souls of heroes. Napoleon appreciated this because he had need of heroes, wherefore he said of Corneille that, if he were still alive, he would have knighted him [*Gespräche mit Goethe in den letzten Jahren seines Lebens, 1823–1832*].

History, particularly in the antique world, conforms entirely to this view of Goethe's. Why then do we doubt it? Because we have every right to doubt it. For the personal experience of each one of us proves today that, after a certain time of life, the drama ceases to exert any influence over us. Sooner or later each of us notices that the stage has left him unsatisfied. He may still go to the theatre, but the big, soul-stirring, primitive excitement gradually ceases, and he becomes sadly convinced that even the works of the greatest dramatists have more effect on him when he enjoys them at home by himself than when he sees them on the stage. At first one thinks: There are no more performers of real talent. But one soon becomes convinced that this is not true. We find great individual performances, perhaps more often now than at any time in the past. And we are moved by them. None of our leading productions is ever so insignificant that it does not offer us solitary beauties, isolated figures, single moments which enchant us. It is the production as a whole that disappoints us. And even in those rare instances in which we feel that the performance in its entirety is stylistically complete, even then a secret voice says to us: That is not our style; that does not belong to us in the same way that a picture by Leibl belongs to us, or a statue by Rodin.

7

It has been the misfortune of various theatre people heretofore that, although honestly partaking of the general distaste for current theatrical practices, they still believed sincerely in the "reform" of existing conditions. Reform, they believed, would lead to Utopia. Since they were in no position to alter the conventional theatre and thus to obtain a type of staging which would have satisfied the more cultivated audiences, they tried to take from the general public a theatre which, on the whole, pleased it. Moreover, such reformers always approached the problems of the theatre from the point of view of one particular art, either literature, or music, or decoration. They never considered the art of the theatre as a synthesis of these various arts, or as a specific art form in itself. For this reason such reformers were doomed to failure from the start.

Every so often reformers would appear who would advocate making the theatre a "center of culture" and assigning to it a place similar to that occupied by the museums. Just as certain examples of plastic art, which have been removed from their original places of usefulness in some church or palace, are preserved in museums for scientific study and for the intellectual enjoyment of a few connoisseurs, so it was suggested that the theatre should serve as a repository for certain examples of poetry, literature, and music. Those who desired this arrangement seem to have forgotten that theatres are capitalistic enterprises like any other and must adapt themselves to the laws of supply and demand. There is no demand from the general public for the production of distinguished poetic dramas, and those of more cultivated taste, who might have an honest desire for such performances, can never be served by the conventional theatre. The conventional theatre must in the main operate so as to satisfy the theatrical taste of the public at large. Therefore, it must present even the greatest of dramatic masterpieces on this cultural level.

It is true that the conventional court theatres and the large civic theatres are required to give performances of the so-called "classics" for the development of the young and the instruction of the masses, who, as recipients of this bounty, we can only pity. Since these institutions are subsidized from public funds, it has seemed desirable that this fiction of idealistic intention be upheld, although everyone knows the real state of affairs.

The conventional theatre cannot produce works of pronounced rhythmical form so that the requirements of good taste are satisfied as they are satisfied by our modern masters of painting, sculpture, architecture, and poetry. The mechanical arrangements of the stage make it impossible. But, under favorable circumstances, what the performances lack as a whole the individual performers sometimes make up for. Such individual performances deserve all the more admiration since they often have to take place in surroundings which are like caricatures of the ideal. If today an educated person leaves the theatre with a feeling of satisfaction, it is due either to the merit of some such unusual artist or to the spectator's own ability to minimize unfavorable impressions. It is a heavy task after the heat and burden of the day to sit through a performance of a worthwhile piece in the conventional theatre. We expect a festival and find only fatigue.

8

Again, let us ask ourselves what we want when we go to the theatre. Goethe said to Eckermann, "There one finds poetry, painting, song, and music; the art of acting and how much more besides! If all these arts and graces, all this beauty and vitality, come together in a single evening and on a high plane, the result is a festival which can be compared with nothing else" (*Gespräche mit Goethe in den letzten Jahren seines Leben, 1823–1832*).

In the rise of the German drama we know that at first there were only traveling mummers. They executed grotesque acrobatics and dancing, sang songs, spoke pieces and dialogues. These activities came down from ancient heathen times and had to do with the celebration of the yearly festivals—the coming of spring, the autumn harvest, the winter solstice, and the like. It has been shown that these mummers' performances, which here and there take place even today, are survivals of ancient festivals of sacrifice. The origin of both comedy and tragedy is the same for German drama as it was for the drama of the Greeks and the Chinese. Tragedy developed as part of religious observances, and comedy grew out of the good-fellowship attending festive occasions.

The Christian church divided these entertainments into carnival and mystery plays. The first of these (*Fastnachtsspiele*) took place in the carnival season, just before Lent. And just as the church took over the heathen festivals and gave them Christian meaning, so it also made use of the drama to heighten the effect of its own religious pomp and ceremony, thus developing the mystery plays.

Our modern theatre is not, however, a continuation of the ancient *Fastnachtsspiele* and certainly not of the mysteries. It dates back to the court celebrations, which, during the sixteenth and seventeenth centuries, were imported from foreign lands.

It would be foolish to attempt here to trace its origins. The centers of culture from which the conventional theatre developed its present form no longer exist. Just as the sham renaissance façades of many of our public buildings are parvenu imitations of ancient palaces, and just as the Renaissance and rococo furnishings of our middle-class houses are poor imitations of court appointments, so the present-day theatre with its boxes and its peep-show stage is not an organic design independently developed, but a crude imitation of the ballet theatres of the baroque courts.

On the other hand, it would be wrong to imagine that our present-day theatres would have pleased the people of that era. The culture of that period had genuine distinction. The present-day commercial theatres are quite unlike the old court theatres even when, as in the case of the *Residenztheater* in Munich, they are installed in ancient buildings. They are still imitations. In the court society of the late Renaissance, of the baroque, the rococo, and even of the Empire periods, the charming little comedy houses that existed were expressions of the social requirements of court society. Their elaborate and artificial decorations, their mechanical contrivances, even their lighting effects, suited the style of their productions.

The bombastic verses, the hoop skirts, beauty patches, and powdered wigs all belonged together.

The installation of the wing stage as a permanent theatrical form came about of necessity. The stabilization of the stage took place a hundred years ago when the mummer bands were invited to install themselves at court, and the players then had to accommodate themselves as best they could to the theatres which already existed in court circles for the presentation of ballet and of opera. The combination of the wing stage and the circular theatre was a makeshift arrangement which became an established institution in spite of the warnings of all the best minds of the times. Goethe, Schiller, Schinkel, Tieck, Immermann, Devrient, and Hoffmann all disapproved of it.

9

We know with certainty that these eminent men, to whom we owe the renaissance of the drama, were never satisfied with the productions which resulted from this makeshift arrangement. In Weimar, Goethe zealously studied theatre construction, hoping to find means to improve it. His efforts were all directed toward freeing the stage from the disadvantages which resulted from that ridiculous combination of opera house and festival hall which was the expedient of the wandering troupes of players.

By examining the history of his productions in Weimar, we discover that here Goethe was actually working toward an ideal which is in harmony with the results obtained at the Artists' Theatre. He knew that the equipment of the stage is a problem in design. He understood that, because of circumstances inherent in the very purpose of the theatre, the solution of this problem should be left entirely in the hands of those who work specifically with matters of design; that is, the architect and painter, in co-operation with the director of the production.

In May 1815, he commented (*To Proserpina*), "One should employ not only those elements which are essentially theatrical, but one should also make use of everything which has been accomplished in the realm of plastic art." Accordingly he demanded that Schinkel and the painter Lütke (a pupil of Hackert) should co-operate so that "the talents of the landscape painter and the architect may be called on jointly."

This is the fundamental idea of the Munich Artists' Theatre. And it is the Munich Artists' Theatre which, a hundred years later, with the use of the technical and artistic methods of the twentieth century, has actually realized the program of Goethe and Schinkel. Goethe knew that the question of design was not a superficial one. He understood that it determines the nature of the drama in so far as the play, the actor, the text—in short, everything that concerns the presentation—is inextricably bound up with the setting in the midst of which the action takes place.

The wing stage was evolved from the practices of the itinerant theatrical companies. These wandering troupes had to take their decoration with them, all neatly rolled up in their wagons. Of such decorations they never had more than five pieces. As the stage became stationary, the wandering players took their ideas of scenery into the court opera and festival houses to which they were now called. They elaborated their decorations somewhat with the idea that, after this fashion, the stage space, which was much too deep for the drama, might be filled.

They did not yet think of creating an illusion of reality. They simply enlarged a little the backdrop, wings, set pieces, and properties which they had used before. And these enlargements were supposed to represent nothing different from what they had formerly represented on the small-scale wagon stages of the traveling players. They made simply a frame for the actors, consisting of things which were essentially suggestions. From these, the imagination of the audience could fill in what was necessary in time and space for the comprehension of the drama.

So the stage conventions continued till the Biedermeier period. They did not show either to realism or to tradition that despicable subservience which expresses itself in imitation with insufficient means. The theatres, scenes, costumes, and furniture of that time proved to be always in harmony with the characteristics of the culture which then existed among the courts, the nobility, and the old *bourgeoisie*. That the theatres then went over to the use of sham materials, and to cheap tinsel, and tawdriness of costume, happened more from poverty than from pleasure in the shams themselves. They simply did not have the money to build stages on which one might give the great works of contemporary masters against rich settings such as the extravagant courts had once furnished for their stern tragedies and loose comedies.

The surrender of the decorous old stage traditions to barbarous theatricalism became absolute when the disorganized and crass *bourgeoisie* of the rising machine civilization tried to outshine the genuine splendor of the court festivities by the use of artifice and sham. Or when, with insane arrogance, they presumed to compete in a peep show with the unbounded exuberance and beauty of nature itself.

With the coming of grand opera the theatre became the stronghold of the most blatant pseudo culture that Europe has ever known. Grand opera was originated for display. The roaring din of its orchestra, the throat-splitting coloratura of its prima donnas, the padded tights of its bombastic virtuosos, and the breath-taking sensationalism of its dramatics were matched by the glittering claptrap of the production, by the auditorium with its circle of boxes filled with ostentatious parvenus, and by the pompous façade with its disfiguring Renaissance decorations. Today the general public makes no secret of the fact that beside grand opera—the music drama of Wagner is identical in their minds with grand opera—every other form of dramatic offering seems insignificant. A theatre which counts with the general public must therefore always take pains to conform in everything, even in its plays, to the conventions of grand opera. From this it follows that a theatre for cultivated people could only develop under conditions which did not depend at all on the general public.

Such conditions came about in Munich. People of taste and culture had become accustomed to congregate there at certain seasons of the year. These are the people who today may be counted on as a reliable and steady public for the Artists' Theatre. They are the people who set standards, and where they go, others will follow. It is an old discovery. One need only announce a thing as exclusive, and the perquisite of the elite, to have it at once in demand, for everyone likes to consider himself among the elite. The effect of this not-at-all unworthy ambition has been notable in the case of the Artists' Theatre. At first many people came because they saw that it was the mode among those who set the fashion. Soon they were themselves converted and came again frequently. What is simple and inevitable is soon accepted.

Today cultivated people are united in the opinion that in the elaborate playhouses with their peep-show stages an artistic production can never be achieved. Anselm Feuerbach spoke for us all when he said, "I hate the modern theatre because I have sharp eyes and cannot be fooled by pasteboard and cosmetics. I despise the absurdity of its decor. It degrades the public, dissipates the last remnant of sound feeling, and begets a barbarous taste which sound art repudiates."

10

The Artists' Theatre should not be considered as a revolt against tradition but, on the contrary, as evidence of our goodly heritage. We merely continue from the point at which our development was interrupted by the Thirty Years' War and other disturbances to our culture. It would obviously be an impoverishing archaism if—as some romanticists demand—we were to introduce the primitive stage conditions of the time of Shakespeare and Hans Sachs without contributing anything further. Such devices would not represent our culture. We shall do better to create that stage which would now be in existence if advancement from the very simple beginnings to the present time had never been interrupted and if, along the way, use had been made of all artistic and technical discoveries as they developed.

For all such activities Munich is the ideal place. Under the thin veneer of the ornate city "with all modern conveniences," Munich has kept alive many of the old traditions. One even finds there a bit of the atmosphere of a peasant village. For, until the modern age of travel pushed open its gates, Munich was really an old Bavarian farming town, as well as the royal grand ducal residence. More of this early atmosphere remains than one would suppose. Therefore, the re-establishment of valid traditions in the way of city building, engineering, household furnishing, decoration, painting, and the use of sculpture in design does not seem nearly so revolutionary or so modern in Munich as elsewhere—for example, in Berlin. In Munich valid artistic principles never actually ceased to exist. Only for a few decades was sound work according to the old traditions less in evidence than were the productions of the upstarts who, with the first high tide of the revolution in the world of mechanical production and capitalistic enterprise, poured over Munich and ravaged it.

Now that period of extravagance is over. Sound principles of art emerge once more—simple, basic, and essential. And we realize that they were always present. Kobell was painting beside Cornelius; Spitzweg beside Kaulbach; beside Piloty, Leibl. And while our magnificent city was being disfigured by bank buildings in the hideous Renaissance style of Berlin's *Friederichstrasse*, Gabriel von Seidl went on building in the good old fashion of his fathers, according to exactly the same principles that are now followed by younger men like Fischer, the Rank brothers, Riemerschmid, and others. In short, the connection between "the good old times" and "the good new times" which bridges the chasm of depravity in taste that obtained from 1850 to 1900 is much closer and more comprehensible in Munich than anywhere else.

So, too, with the theatre. Even though the official theatres of the town follow the Berlin and Viennese custom of literary and commercial theatricalism, many connections with the folk drama remain unbroken in Munich today. The old music halls preserved their charm and their integrity. The Puppet Theatre is still carried on today by "Papa" Schmidt in the center of old Munich just as it was when Count Pocci raised it from the fairs and markets of Upper Bavaria and gave it literary interest. The Puppet Theatre of the Munich Artists, which was established by Paul Brann and known as an enterprise similar to that of the Artists' Theatre, is descended directly from the tradition of Pocci-Schmidt. Its character was developed by such Munich artists as Taschner, Bradl, and Salzmann in the spirit of the Punch and Judy shows which are to be found in all Bavarian market places and church festivals.

But the close relationship between the Munich Artists' Theatre and the ancient theatrical culture becomes even clearer if we go outside the gates of Munich. Not very far, only to Dachau. At this place there have been since ancient times a Passion play and Manger plays of the Three Wise Men. These last have been performed again by Munich artists after an intermission of more than a hundred years. The most amazing thing about the revival of these ancient and traditional manger plays is that one feels as though they had always existed—as though they belonged to the land and to the people. I saw them on New Year's Day in 1905.

There lay the little town before us glimmering in the icy winter air, rising above the snowy moor that farther off was lost in the blue haze of the horizon. We tramped through the snow and up the mountain to which the houses cling between the rushing rivulets of the Amper, as though seeking anxiously for support and protection. Suddenly the outline of the mountain stood out from the moor, and against it gleamed the white castle, lit by the sharp rays of the winter sun. On we went past the church and through the broad main street, which winds along with an air of ancient dignity. Here the gabled houses stand like the worthy members of a town meeting, stern and important, side by side. Beautiful old emblems on wrought iron standards hang over the street, and the town well is carefully wrapped up for the winter.

The door at the entrance to the castle courtyard was decorated with evergreens and above in the middle hung a great gold paper star. Young girls in their Sunday best, peasant boys in high boots, pale nuns, and jovial churchmen entered with us. In the room above, the windows were covered and the lights were lit. The galleries and the walls below them were decorated with green branches. Here were crowded the people of Dachau and a few visitors from Munich, most of them artists. The atmosphere was hushed, as in a church.

Finally it grew dark and the music began. Between evergreens a curtain drew apart, and there appeared a forge at which a man with sinewy arms was engaged in heavy work with glowing iron. Women and children stood about, the red light of the fire playing strangely on their solemn faces. Mankind was at work in the drab, monotonous Everyday. There was no attempt to make the walls appear as anything other than what they were, merely simple draperies. There was nothing of the genre or anecdotal, as in the theatre. And so everything that was universal and essential became significant. The "voices from on high" rang out with joy, and as the simple people in the hut looked up, the firelight from the hearth glowed on their lips and was reflected in their eyes. This common gesture of looking aloft gave a marvelously strong impression of trust and longing.

Gray-violet hangings enclosed the next scene like the snow-laden sky of a dull winter evening. In front of these were placed pines and fir trees, with here and there the silver-white of a birch sapling and branches to which the brown autumn foliage was still clinging. Nothing more was needed to give the amosphere of a winter landscape. Far off, candlelight gleamed through the branches, and in the foreground three shepherd lads lay around a fire. They passed the tedious watches of the night with various jokes. The faces, the gestures, the speech were typically those of Dachau. There was a harmony throughout that was a joy to see. No one could be out of character because everything that was done was developed according to the ways and customs of the land.

There was an impressive moment when St. Joseph, played by a grown man, joined the shepherd boys, for he was much, much larger than the shepherds, really as though of another dimension. This was stylistically a splendid touch and was strengthened by the fact that St. Joseph spoke high German—not the same speech as the common people.

The next scene was ushered in with martial music. Through the hall, through the midst of the audience, came the Three Kings, one of them a pitch-black man from the country of the Moors, carrying an enormous lantern. They advanced searching over the land for the newborn king, concerning whom they had received a prophecy.

But the guiding star—a Christmas-tree star which an angel carried on a stick, as a proper star ought to be carried—led them not into a royal palace but into a manger. There in the last picture the Baby lay on the hay while beside Him knelt His Mother in devotion and humility. And round about stood the angel children and St. Joseph. The expression of the Virgin Mary was indescribably moving in its simple dignity.

The scenic problem of the manger was well solved. Here, obviously, there could be no competition with nature. There could not be, as often happens in the conventional theatre, a true-to-nature manger spirited in by trickery, a manger in whose realness no one believes. But the most natural thing was to do as the old masters did with the mangers in their paintings—that is, to include only such outlines as represented the traditional qualities of a manger. In this case, it was more like a piece of crumbled masonry with rafters and stark bulk somewhat enlarged. The result was charming. Nowhere was there any sham or artifice. The angels wore no tinsel, tights, or make-up. No gold-paper wings were pasted on their shoulders. They simply stood there solemnly as before a miracle.

And herein may lie the incomparable effect of such productions. For these children, the performance is something tremendous which takes place to the glory of God, a wonder that quickens their pulses and fires their imagination. For this reason there is a brightness shining in their eyes and a tremble in their childish voices. It was quite unnecessary to put them into costumes. In their everyday garments, many in the poorest smocks and barefoot, others in their Sunday best, they were arranged by a painter with an understanding of color harmonies, and they looked so beautiful that one inevitably thought of Dürer and Schöngauer—particularly in the last picture when each in his own fashion, but quite uncoached, showed reverence to the Child. Here one could see that there is much native beauty, natural style, and fullness of expression in gesture and in movement which our people possess but which, so far, has never been properly nurtured and developed for the stage.

During the following years the Manger plays were again produced, this time in Munich itself. Otto Falckenberg obtained the original peasant texts, Bernard Stavenhagen composed the music, and the sculptor Georg Schreyözz helped them to create an architectural frame for the play in the ancient Gothic rooms of the old Town Hall. He also helped them to design the costumes and arrange the groupings. The result was a vision which made the beholder feel as if here, under the darkening roof between the guild flags and the studded oaken doors, such plays had always gone on. The clownlike Moorish slaves of Herod seemed to be blood brothers of the grotesque dancing figures carved on the cornice of the ancient council hall. Yet there was no archaism. Electric light was skillfully employed, and there was never anything self-consciously primitive or picturesquely quaint about the style of the production. The actress who played Mary, Frau Greiner-Urfus, who came from the Reinhardt school, was very effective, as was the entire production, which may, after a fashion, be counted as a forerunner of the Artists' Theatre.

We may see this impressive type of old German theatrical production in many places in Bavaria where the Passion plays have been put on with a continuity of tradition. Oberammergau is of course world-famous. But there unfortunately we find the original style of scene design and decoration spoiled by the introduction of opera machinery. Eduard Devrient saw the Oberammergau players in 1850 in their original form and came to the conclusion that this tradition would survive.

In his writings on the Oberammergau Passion Play, to which he owes his world-wide reputation, he also says, "The Munich October Festival may someday be the source of the first great historical theatre." By this he meant the performance of classical dramas in artistically simplified settings. "The strength and talent for this enterprise may be found in two sources: first, in the university with its various schools; and second, in the association of workers in the plastic arts."

So, more than half a century ago, Eduard Devrient designated Munich as the place where artists, working together with the other cultural factors, would realize the ideal of a festival house for the German drama in a form at once artistic and popular.

Even in details Devrient foresaw the future accurately —for example, in his reference to the university. The Artists' Theatre has received warm encouragement from prominent persons in the field of education. Many students and teachers have worked in the chorus of the theatre. Moreover, the movement of the chorus perpetuated an old Bavarian art—a relief style after the character of ancient German woodcarvings. By means of an entirely modern handling of form we achieved, quite without conscious intention, a result which was fully in harmony with the old traditions.

From what has already been said, it is obvious that the architectural and decorative principles of the Artists' Theatre are founded on the work of such men as Schinkel, Hoffmann, Immermann, and Semper. We are not upstarts without traditions or inheritance. On the contrary. What we are opposing is the lack of taste and style which has been part of a period of specious culture. The overthrow of these false standards in every department of life is the chief task of our times.

II

Although the scenic decoration of the stage is not the most important point to be considered, it offers the most palpable means of showing the need for a new theatre. In the average theatre of today stage decoration is usually reminiscent of the historical paintings and genre pictures of the sixties and seventies—and on that level it has been obliged to remain. The impossible perspective of the peep show, the all-revealing illumination of the footlights, the unreality of the material make the development of genuine decorative art impossible. The best that the peep-show theatre has to offer has been given us by the Meiningen Theatre. The elaborate stage pictures of the Meiningen productions are about on a par with the works of Piloty. No type of staging has ever gone farther in this direction —not even Wagner.

It is well known that Richard Wagner intended to have Böcklin design the scenery for his music dramas. As Wagner pondered the stage pictures for the *Ring*, he said, "This would be something for Böcklin! He alone possesses sufficient imagination." But a single sketch for the dragon Fafner was all the Swiss painter contributed. Wagner and Böcklin could work no further together. For Wagner, as Ostini reported,[7] made technical demands which Böcklin considered artistically impossible. And Böcklin was right. Wagner clung to the peep-show stage, with its footlights and stage machinery, and shut out thereby the conception of the painter in the true and artistic meaning of the word.

So, in the end, Wagner gained nothing from calling upon Böcklin beyond the fact that the latter often asserted that Wagner knew nothing of painting. It must have seemed an absurdity to Böcklin to be expected to attain unity of design through false lighting in an impossible perspective—to say nothing of the relation of such arbitrary factors to the actual and fixed dimensions of the human figure which inevitably was part of the whole design.

The conventional peep-show stage gives us decorative and scenic depth without being able in any way to make the human figure correspondingly smaller against this depth. And at the same time it claims vociferously that it is "true to nature." The performer appears at a distance of ten or twenty meters from the footlights exactly as large and as clear in detail as at the very footlights. And yet, according to the proportions of scene painting, he should be much farther off and should be perceived, if he is to appear in proper relation to the surrounding trees, houses, and mountains, as a greatly diminished object, as a small silhouette, if not indeed as a mere speck.

It is not just a question of the fine points of technique involved in painting and design. The worst painting of the poorest period of German artistic decline is, in all these respects, more satisfactory than the most pretentious stage picture that was ever conjured up on the peep-show stage. For even a well-painted perspective becomes artistically impossible when the relations of the wing set and the footlights are false to each other. The conventional theatre counts on the inability of the audience to retain visual impressions with any certainty, on the grotesque inexactness of all memory pictures, and on the neglect of eye training which characterized the older generation in Germany before 1900.

Today cultivated people are all acquainted with modern painting. And they have some knowledge of ancient art as well. No theatre can offer such audiences the various atrocities which were accepted by the older generation, a generation which did not even look upon nature, to say nothing of pictures, with their eyes, but only with their reason and their "feelings."

Theatres which served the more highly cultivated public recognized this fact. Even in the presentation of the most naturalistic pieces, the peep show had already proved useless. Theatrical directors were often forced to circumvent the restrictions of the wing stage by building various devices. Even for naturalism the old-fashioned theatre was an incubus which was stupidly endured only because there seemed to be no architects, painters, or designers who could create a stage to satisfy modern standards.

Yet at this very time great artists existed, artists in whom were united all of those gifts from which the art of decorative painting has developed, artists, some of whom disappeared either unrecognized or repudiated and whose fate is a disgrace to our people. But in that time of barbarism those among us who were most gifted had least influence. Certainly their ideas were not accepted in the theatre. The public could not bring itself to part from the peep show with its cardboard scenery and fake romanticism. It would not even give up the footlights, although electric light could illuminate the stage from all directions. In the age of the tallow candle and the oil lamp it had of course been necessary for the convenience of the lamplighter to have steps leading up to the stage. Even these were kept. A reaction set in only when the theatre could sink no lower, when it became so perverted that it represented the exact opposite of its real purpose, spirit, and style, when it had become merely a repository for literature.

In demanding a stage decoration that is true to nature, naturalism demonstrated that the sleight-of-hand mechanics of the conventional theatre, which have been elevated almost to the rank of a science, are absurd. This demonstration is naturalism's most valuable accomplishment. Formerly, when meagre childish suggestions and simple aids to the imagination were all that was expected, illusion on the peep-show stage was much more easily attained. Then it did not matter if the rocky walls sometimes showed creases or if an actor occasionally reached for a chair that was only painted on the wall. But now, when everything even to the smallest detail must be represented with the greatest physical exactness, now, when one continually examines everything in the light of reality, the gentlest breeze playing across surfaces that are ostensibly of stone suffices to make the whole technique ridiculous. And so this complicated, expensive apparatus, that has as its sole purpose the creation of a perfect illusion of reality, can never be successful. The more it is elaborated and expanded, the more it shows its weakness.

The perfection of naturalism by mechanical means has developed the peep show *ad absurdum*. We have come to the end of our wisdom. The conventional theatre itself has proved to us that we are encumbered with an apparatus that prohibits all healthy growth. This whole sham world of cardboard, twine, canvas, and gilt is ripe for destruction.

II

The Function and Style of the Stage

One of our most distinguished jurists has written a famous book called *The Function of Law.* Perhaps some artist-philosopher of the future may write a book entitled *The Function of Art.* Function dictates the form of social existence, and that is law. But function also establishes the form of artistic creation, and that is style. If we wish to gain insight into an artistic phenomenon, we must first of all investigate its function.

As we have already seen, the function of the stage is to stimulate and to satisfy an overpowering expectation. If we are so aroused that within the confines of convention we can not completely realize this emotion, we must rise above conventions, above reality, into a cosmos in which the world (which we have never actually apprehended as a unit but have only glimpsed in fragments) is suddenly revealed to us as a complete and perfect pattern. This is the function of all art; it is particularly the function of the stage. In the theatre mankind should meet the ultimate in both good and evil.

Aesthetic satisfaction results from such an intensification of our existence as it is the function of the theatre to supply. This fulfillment is an experience the vividness of which is in direct proportion to the degree to which we are compelled, by the suggestion exerted in the rhythmic force inherent in the drama itself, to participate emotionally in the action upon the stage. Here we drink life much more deeply than we have the opportunity to do in the ordinary workaday world. This was known to Aristotle, whose "catharsis" is literally a purging, a relaxation of our life forces in a complete fulfillment of ourselves, as in a kind of higher chorus.

We have already admitted that we do not go to the theatre to find literature, music, or art. We go there to experience emotion shared in common with our fellows. But to have this experience we must be swept along together in the same irresistible current. This mutual perception begins for us when on entering the theatre we greet one another, stroll up and down, chat, joke, laugh. We are swept into a stronger current the moment a performer steps forward and concentrates our attention upon himself and then, by some sort of rhythmical expression, moves our hearts and minds in a certain definite cadence.

The actor's immediate means to this end is his own body. Dramatic art is, in its own way, dancing, that is, rhythmic movement of the human body in space. It is an example of the individual's creative urge toward harmonious participation in a universal experience. Through the dance his personal experience is beneficently, even intoxicatingly, apprehended as part of a Perfect Order, a state superior to reality.

The dance has always been a cultural form. Among the ancients it was in fact the most important of all cultural forms. The holiest of all mysteries is the sacrifice which, considered as form, is the apex of all dance technique. (Even today in the religious dances of savage peoples the sacrifice is so interpreted.) And out of this technique has grown our conception of tragedy. As the movement of the performer becomes more lively, rhythms appear of themselves. The stamping of the feet is audible in a certain beat, the hands move and clap in regular time, and finally this violent movement wrings sounds from the panting breast of the performer: a croak, a hiss, a groan, a sigh. These rhythmical sounds—expressions of feeling, utterances of passion, and the like—were gradually and consciously cultivated and finally became song. They evolved into the rhythmical accompaniment of spoken words. Then came the poet to elevate this rhythmical sequence of tones or words into the spiritual world of the drama. And it should always be remembered that a drama which is genuine in style can only develop if the poet responds to the rhythms of the festival crowd itself. During the process of creation he experiences such movement only in his imagination, but it is always there and will instinctively be divined by the performers and ultimately by the audience. Everything else is literature; as such, it may be a classic, but it is not drama.

I shall not dwell further on the way in which, out of the festival crowd thus inspired by the performer, a group of those who are most strongly moved will gradually break away. This group, feeling itself drawn into a closer communion with the performer, becomes a chorus, encouraging him by clapping and by cries and finally by grasping musical instruments in order to excite him more and more. Thus the orchestra develops. At last, torn from this smaller circle by the power of the actor's hypnotic rhythms, single individuals are drawn to him and forced into the action as fellow players. All that is important for us here to remember is that the drama, even in its most complicated and intellectual form, is basically the same as it was in its earliest beginnings, that is to say, rhythmic movement of the human body in space, movement that has developed naturally from the movement of a festival crowd.

Taine says of Hellenic culture, "Man was moulded by the chorus. It taught him a pliable carriage, gestures, and movement. It placed him in a group which was a plastic relief; it made him an involuntary actor." And, furthermore, we should never forget that the drama, according to its basic nature, is one with the festival crowd. For it exists only if the crowd experiences it. "The circumstance of the dramatic experience is the determining truth"; these words of Adolf von Hildebrand go to the root of the matter. But some of our philosophers, when discussing art in the superficial fashion in which they are accustomed to consider it, have maintained that a work of art is an objective thing, existing for its own sake. This is obviously a ridiculous delusion.

2

A work of art has in itself no more value than the material of which it is composed. A poem, though it be the creation of the greatest poet, if it is written in a language which no living man can understand, is nothing more than a piece of paper. The value, therefore, is not in the work of art. It may be assessed only when man comes in contact with it, when it becomes the experience of some human being. This contact releases in that human being some sort of rhythmic reaction—and this reaction is the only real artistic value that exists. It is the beginning and the end of all art. A work of art only has value in so far as it calls forth such a reaction and only so long as that reaction is in effect. The artistic value is recreated every time it is experienced. What we call "art" or "beauty" is neither object nor is it subject, but rather it is reaction, the contact of the subject with the object and the mastery by the subject of the object. The reaction is realized, is raised to consciousness, through certain organs that we generally describe as "mind" or "spirit." It depends on the nature of these organs how many of such vibrations are received and with what intensity, how frequently and how vigorously by their obedience to rhythmic law they are felt by the individual as harmony and concord, filling him with the joy that comes from the recognition of perfection.

That the experience of those who sit before the stage is not identical with that which takes place upon the stage itself is readily established. The artistic reality (which is purely an activity of the spirit) is in no way identical with the "real" reality of the stage happenings and appearances. It is not necessary to prove this to anyone. And yet it is quite frequently forgotten when there is discussion of the drama, of actors, of the stage, of scenery, or of direction. No one should ever attempt to identify the dramatic work of art with the happenings on the stage and apart from the audience to consider it as a thing in itself. For it is in the audience that the dramatic work of art is actually born—born at the time it is experienced—and it is *differently* experienced by every individual member of the audience. The beginning of a dramatic work of art is not upon the stage or even in a book. It is created at that moment when it is experienced as movement of form in time and space.

Everything that either consciously or unconsciously influences the individual contributes in some fashion to this experience: first of all, the actual instigator of the dramatic phenomenon, the actor; next, the area in which he acts and his relation in space to the participating spectators; all the contributing factors, both optical and acoustic; everyone's physical and mental climate and well-being—in short, everything in the total situation. Nothing is unimportant that influences the situation at this moment. The task of artists in the theatre is to sort out from this intricate mass of impressions, influences, and potentialities the most significant, to find how each may be utilized to promote the development of the drama, and to shape all arrangements accordingly. Whether one needs to consider a very wide range of influences or only a restricted one depends on the nature and the general degree of cultural advancement.

We know that the contemporaries of Hans Sachs and of Shakespeare accepted conditions which, with the exception of the performers and the words, were extremely crude. The environment of the actors, the characteristic designations of the stage, their own comfort as regards seating, warmth, ventilation, and lines of vision—all these were unimportant to the people of that time. But they nevertheless achieved the desired aesthetic experience.

The antique world was different. The Greeks and the Romans of the highest cultural development expected the theatre building and the scenic background of the play to contribute to the artistic effect of the whole production, so that the dramatic experience might enter the soul with such force and purity as to engender a complete and satisfactory artistic impression. This was true in the Renaissance and in the period of rococo, and it is true today. Every era of culture develops those forms and conventions that are best suited to the reception of the dramatic experience in exactly the way most appropriate to its own especial spirit. These forms are continually changing and replacing one another.

The last of such changes in Germany were those made by the Meiningen school. The Meiningen players developed a technique of dramatic production which included everything that was necessary to give their particular audience complete satisfaction. This audience consisted of a *bourgeoisie* which was entirely rationalistic in spirit. They had great respect for historical and scientific authenticity, and by their rather naïve minds such authenticity was accepted as "realism"—first, as "historical" realism and then as "modern" realism. That they labeled this "modern" realism specifically as "naturalism" in opposition to the realism which they called "historical" was fundamentally illogical, for the one is as "natural" as the other. Whether one copies a Romanesque church or a modern drawing room, a Merovingian coronation robe or a machine-made blouse, the principle is the same. Modern naturalism was merely the final step in the historical method of the Meiningen Theatre.

And this method was the right one for the general public of that time, for it satisfied them so completely that they once more embraced the drama as a great experience. It is significant, too, that in the form of the auditorium they still clung to the fiction of playing before a magnificent court society. Indeed, some such illusion was indispensable if the drama was to impress that parvenu and bourgeois audience. And so one comes to understand why, in those elaborate theatres patterned after the festival halls of the baroque and rococo courts, the most sordid and banal of naturalistic performances were given. It was because both the artificiality in the auditorium and the "naturalism" on the stage were necessary in order to give this particular audience a satisfactory dramatic experience.

The step from such theatrical reform to that of the Artists' Theatre was merely the inevitable result of a certain intellectual and cultural change that had taken place in the meantime. Little by little it became apparent that, even though the greatest dramas were played by the most able performers under the most careful direction, thousands and tens of thousands no longer found any satisfaction in the theatre. People of taste were estranged because the theatre lacked certain facilities for winning their allegiance. And those who were most estranged were precisely the most cultivated and the most artistic. It was not merely a matter of the more or less tasteful arrangement of the auditorium, scenery, costumes, and the like. It was a question of the actual survival of the essential quality of the theatre, a question as to whether such people as contribute most to the culture of the nation should have an opportunity to enjoy the drama. Under such conditions as existed in the conventional theatre not even the literati could still take pleasure in the drama. A shifting of cultural emphasis had taken place in which the theatre did not share, and, therefore, there was lacking that sympathetic understanding which must exist in some measure between the minds, instincts, thoughts, and subconscious spiritual forces of the spectators and the events taking place upon the stage.

According to their nature and their origin, player and spectator, stage and auditorium are not in opposition. They are a unit. The Japanese theatre preserves this unity by means of the bridge across which the actor comes forward to the stage from the auditorium itself. Shakespeare's actors were often surrounded by spectators. Also, in the old Italian, French, and German theatres, the most important guests sat right and left of the proscenium so that the actors' chief entrances were made between them. One may say that the unity of the festival crowd—the players and the spectators, the auditorium and the stage—was only lost when, with the fall of ancient cultures, the sensitive appreciation of the real function of the stage passed away, and other crass and pedantic developments took its place.

3

How did the theatre evolve? How did the stage arise as a stylistic concept? The answer is simple. It arose from the fact that the elements of the dramatic experience were assembled in one place. The feet of the dancers—the performers—trod the ground. This resulted in a sort of threshing floor; then, for the convenience of the performers, this space was covered with mats or boards. At the same time stationary seats were built for the comfort of the spectators, and as the number of spectators increased, it became necessary to raise the playing space. The stage had arrived! Simultaneously, and for the same reason, the seats of the spectators at the back of the circle were elevated; the amphitheatre was created. In principle, the theatre was complete. Everything that has been added is secondary—additions which were introduced because of climatic conditions and other subordinate circumstances. That the raised stage was finally withdrawn from the center and removed to a segment of the circle happened only as a concession to the convenience of the performers.

In considering the form of the stage in relation to its function, we must realize that the theatre is not merely an eclectic work of art. It does not attain perfection solely as a synthesis of all the other arts, but as an art in itself. It has different purposes and origins and also different laws and privileges than the other arts. It does not need the other arts in order to exist. The drama is possible without word or tone, without scenery or costume, simply as rhythmic movement of the human body; but the art of the stage can enrich its rhythms and its forms from the wealth of all other arts. And since, as we have seen, the function of the theatre is to be a festival meeting place for a common cultural life, enrichment of the stage will follow the general enrichment of culture. But if the drama is to draw additional strength of expression from the other arts, it is obvious that it must place poetry, music, painting, and architecture under dramatic regulation without forcing them to repudiate the innate principles of their individual arts.

III

The Actor

THE valuable talents of our modern actors are being wantonly wasted. Theatrical performers have not even been able to consolidate such slight advances toward the elevation of their art as were begun by Goethe. All natural freedom of physical expression has been denied them, and like monkeys they have been trained to ape the empty chatter and inane behavior of the everyday world. One is oppressed by the feeling that soon it will be impossible to find an actor who can still speak German dramatic verse in a manner suitable to the stage.

If we disregard the current crop of cheap buffoonery and silly slapstick and turn our attention only to such modern pieces as are well above the average in literary merit, what do we find? Plays that require the actor to smoke, spit, cough, snort, sniffle, belch, and hawk; to have at the tip of his tongue a disgusting gibberish of dialects and obsolete expressions; to be able to reproduce in his person a fleeting fragment of the accidental and the obvious so that those of vulgar and complacent mind may sigh, "Ah! such is life!"

But cultivated people have ceased to take pleasure in imitation of the accidental. The leaders of German culture long ago advanced the other arts—music, sculpture, painting, architecture, and decoration—beyond imitation and beyond naturalism. They have rejected such performances as cling to confused, undisciplined techniques. Today young actors are not infrequently surpassed in the control of their bodies and in all the physical principles of their art by singers, dancers, and even by the buffoons of burlesque. And for this reason painters and other artists often prefer the genuine technical achievements of the music halls to the ungainly ineptitudes of the theatre.

It is the actor, however, who deserves to occupy the most important place in the theatre. It is he who makes the drama come alive. His art is more important and more significant than has been acknowledged. When he employs his own body—activated by poetic rhythms—for a complete characterization, a perfect fulfillment of humanity, he breaks down a thousand inhibitions. He introduces the dramatist's meaning directly into the consciousness of the audience. And in return for this the audience gives him its deepest devotion. Even when he portrays such villainous parts as Shakespeare's Richard III, the audience loves him. Because although Richard inspires horror, he is subject to the inexorable power of justice.

Audiences love an actor who can give complete physical expression to intellectual and emotional concepts. Everything that is idealistic as well as everything that is sensuous in human beings responds to the actor's art—

everything in woman which is womanly and maternal, everything in man which is powerful and passionate is stimulated and refreshed. To the audience the actor symbolizes the highest aspirations of mankind incorporated in the flesh and moving at the will of the poet.

Therefore the components of the actor's art are vitally important. He must first have perfect command of the words of the poet both in speech and in spirit—he must make them his own. But this is only the beginning. Next he must create. Out of his own being he must create in substance and in truth the figure the poet designates. He must do this not by degrading that creation to the individual and the accidental, but by raising himself to the universal and the absolute. For this achievement the actor's entire body is required. It is a mistake to suppose that the face is the most important area of expression. If the bourgeois device of opera glasses could be eliminated, actors would no longer strive to make "characteristic" grimaces. They would expand their means of expression to fill a larger space. The art of the actor suffers severely if by inartistic direction the performer is restricted to the hampered movements of everyday life.

Even the orator can scarcely restrain his innate desire for a freer idiom of gesture and of movement. For the actor, this desire is the vehicle of all creation. Remember that the actor's art has its origin in the dance. The means of expression used by dancers are also those most natural to the actor. The technique of the actor differs from that of the dancer only in that it possesses greater potentialities for expression. The closer the actor comes to the rhythmically controlled play of the limbs as in the dance, the more creative he can be, even if he never quite becomes a dancer. It is the duty of the dramatic poet to prepare the way for him. Shakespeare's Hamlet is an admirable example of such preparation. To play this role correctly, the actor must interpret spiritual values by the physical medium of the dance. Every word that issues from Hamlet's mouth sends vibrations through his entire body. Watch him with Ophelia. They advance and retreat. They evade one another and come close together. Now they seem to grasp each other and then, dismayed, to spring apart. It is almost a minuet.

OPHELIA: Good my lord,
How does your honor for this many a day?
HAMLET: I humbly thank you; well, well, well.

So begins the formal dance with courteous bows. And herein lies the secret of the greatest roles: Hamlet, Mephistopheles, and all other figures that are created according to the physical nature of the actor's art—out of the dance!

2

Nevertheless, the dance is not in itself the art of acting. It is only the physical force behind it. Acting must first be enriched by the creative values of the imagination and by the fullness of spiritual life. Fortunately, we need not speculate about the stylistic relationship between the dance and the art of acting. This has been illuminated for us by the dancing of Madeleine.[1]

If we still regard this remarkable woman as a phenomenon it can only be as an artistic and cultural phenomenon. The condition of hypnosis is now recognized. Before Madeleine began to dance she had been "put to sleep." But there is nothing phenomenal in this; it is not even unusual. All artists who appear in public, in so far as they are really creative artists under the pressure of an inner experience, need "a suggestion," as present-day physicians say. In time each one develops his own special technique of autosuggestion. It is well known that many of the most distinguished never go on without certain small aids. One cannot overcome stage fright without a glass of champagne. Another uses other means to allay the feeling of constraint that oppresses anyone who, before an audience, is expected to disclose his inmost consciousness and to surrender his body for the revelation of secrets that otherwise all his instincts, emotions, and habits command him to conceal. In the case of Madeleine, hypnosis rendered this service, and the slight hysteria that the doctors diagnosed in her proves nothing against her.

It is precisely those people with strong emotions who are most subject to hysteria. This is illustrated by the frenzy of the Corybantes and the bacchantes and other participants in the Dionysian mysteries in the antique world and in the Middle Ages of the flagellants. But Madeleine embodied for us a new type of pantomime and dancing. Never before has the miracle of the transfiguration of mankind, the consummation of pain and pleasure, been brought so clearly before our eyes. She "sleeps," she has no will, no calculation. In utter purity there rises from the well of her soul, stirring its secret depths, creative powers called forth by commanding rhythms. Like the pinion of the angel at the pool of Bethesda, so the melodies sweep across the surface of her spirit. She trembles, she sways, her body moves in delicate waves, surging forward like the surf of the sea driven by the flood tide to ebb again into quiet, peace, and stillness. And what happens here in the dark land, in the unexplored, is clearly reflected before our enchanted eyes. "What in the labyrinth of the heart wanders through the night" emerges through her into the light of day. All this, of course, would not be possible if the grace of creation did not dwell within her. We know only too well that not every woman under the influence of hypnosis would be able to equal her. We cannot doubt her creative gift.

Every work of art is conceived in a sort of somnambulism. Far removed from all calculation, every art form first lives in the soul of the one who creates it. But to bring it forth, to produce it as a work of art, has always in addition required conscious action. And each such conscious process takes from the Eternal something of its completeness, giving an opportunity for human thoughts and purposes to blur the process, giving power to the accidental. Not so here. By metaphysical command the body of Madeleine is exempt from physical laws. Her flesh and blood become part of the universal. *Alles Vergängliche ist nur ein Gleichnis.* (All that is mortal is but an image.)

She is Eve, who offers the apple, artlessly listening to the whispers of temptation, and at the same time she herself is all enticement, all fascination, all destruction. She is Judith, who languishes with lustful anguish in the arms of Holofernes, and who, holding his head aloft by the hair, strides in triumph through the ranks of rejoicing warriors. She is the angel bearing a lily, who brings glad tidings to the Chosen One. She is herself the Blessed Virgin, who receives the benediction humbly and with ecstasy. Now bowed by the weight of grief, she bears in her arms the body of her Son. Now she arises rejoicing, floating in glory at the right hand of God.

There is hardly a tragic figure to which Madeleine has not given shape. As though the beautiful statues of Tanagra had been conjured into life, a procession of grace, love, caprice, desire, and exaltation passes before our eyes.

This was great dramatic art. Perhaps such art was first evoked when Aeschylus conjured the Erinyes out of the night and when Euripides unchained the bacchantes. Here too was a great pictorial art. Indeed, Hellenic art of the great age is no longer a mystery to us. The ancients had just such dancers. All their records tell us of a Dionysian intoxication, of an unquestionably somnambulistic state, on the part of their religious dancers. They often saw what for the first time we have experienced in the dancing of Madeleine. Such control of the corporal body, such creative movement through the power of the spirit, was common to them.

Furtwängler says, "Greek art would be unimaginable without Greek gymnastics." And the dance was a Greek gymnastic art of the period; it united gymnastics with another cultural form, that is, with music. Hence its immense importance in Hellenic civilization. Its importance is of such magnitude that one is forced to conclude that a true culture without the art of the dance, and without education for the dance, would be impossible. Plastic art and drama would always be limited and inadequate without them.

In *Wilhelm Meisters Lehrjahre* Goethe recognized the fact that acting and dancing are kindred arts and demand the same preparation. In *Wilhelm Meisters Wanderjahre* there are passages discussing this theory. For instance, in the third chapter of the third book, as an explanation of Meister's studies of anatomy, we find the following:

> During my theatrical experience I made considerable progress in the understanding of the human body. Observing closely, one sees that in the theatre the physical being plays the leading part. A handsome man, a beautiful woman! If the director is lucky enough to possess these assets, he will soon find dramatic poets. The freer relations in which such a society lives render its members more acquainted with the beauties of the undraped limbs than in any other circumstances.

Moreover, Goethe felt that an education in dancing and gymnastics was valuable in other ways. His purpose was to permeate all life with creative harmonies and rhythms, and to this end it seemed imperative to make gymnastics a basic part of education. In describing the "pedagogical province" in the second book of the *Wanderjahre*, Goethe definitely fixed the place of the dance. He writes,

> Now a stranger would soon notice that, the farther he advanced into this land, the more clearly he would hear the sound of singing. Whatever the youths were doing, with whatever work they were occupied, they always sang. And the songs they sang were always peculiarly suited to the business in which they were engaged. Toward evening dancers appeared, their dancing always enlivened and controlled by the rhythms of the choruses.

Furthermore, his rules for actors are based upon the elements of the dance. Like all great drama, the second part of Goethe's *Faust* is chiefly choreographic in construction. This is also true of the antique tragedies and comedies. In these the dance was the fundamental element determining the style.

There is great significance in Furtwängler's pronouncement, "Greek gymnastics developed at exactly the same period as did the drama." In the same way both teach the cultivation of the body and the physical forms of expression. Anyone who cannot appreciate dancing will be unable really to understand either comedy or tragedy. In our time, however, many educated people have only a literary or intellectual interest in dramatic art. They do not rightly understand nor properly appreciate either the work of our best modern dramatists or that of the great masters of the past, particularly that of Shakespeare. The cultivation of the dance is for many reasons the essential foundation for an education in the art of acting and the drama. On careful consideration it will become obvious that a performer is qualified to bring order out of the chaos of the world by the cultivation of artistic forms only after he has already succeeded in bringing that which is closest and most personal to him—his own body—under the discipline of rhythm and so developed it into a means of expression.

3

The art of dancing and the playing of comedies must again become a sport generally and enthusiastically engaged in. This is important for the physical development of the race. Furthermore, it may result in the reappearance of an audience which is discriminating in regard to the mimic art. For a time the appreciation of the quality of acting almost disappeared. Even among the guild of theatrical critics, there are in Germany today only isolated persons who consider the actor first of all in relation to his acting—as one customarily judges the painter by the particular quality of his painting, the sculptor by nothing except the plastic quality of his work, the builder by his architectural and the musician by his musical qualities alone.

The educated public is so impressed by the printed word that it has accepted the judgment of the critics who evaluate actors only according to literary and psychological standards, although in the plastic arts the public has been encouraged to go in exactly the opposite direction—away from the literary and psychological point of view to the purely aesthetic. If we look back two generations, we find that understanding of the true quality of acting and genuine cultivation of the dance came to an end at about the same time. In the days of our grandparents' youth, when tasteful cultivation of the social dances was still prized, when Pepita and Taglioni were acclaimed, one found everywhere friends of the theatre who could appreciate and judge the quality of acting for its own sake. In this art, as in other arts, the activity of the amateur that is begun as a sport or as a pastime may ultimately develop into a sort of preparatory school from which the more gifted may graduate into mastery of the art. Those not so qualified can, nevertheless, win sufficient technical knowledge to understand and enjoy the ability of the more masterly.

This exercise of the mimic art for personal pleasure was in earlier days a common custom. At the time of the miracle and mystery plays the practice of acting was almost universal, and remnants of this usage are still to be found in our mountain villages even today. Also, acting was encouraged with great intelligence by the Jesuits, and it has been most successfully employed in the education of our nobility. The practice of acting still flourished during Goethe's youth, and its cultivation at the court of Weimar resulted in some of our greatest dramatic poetry: *Iphigenie, Tasso, Die Natürliche Tochter, Faust.* So we see that here again we are merely reviving an old tradition. Such practice in the art of acting as took place at Weimar resulted in the creation of dramas that have become the common property of our entire race. Perhaps in the future under similar circumstances something of the sort may again occur.

To this end all our endeavor should be directed. This art belongs to the whole people or it is nothing. It would be ridiculous in our democratic times to consider only the desires of a few dilettantes. Anyone who really knows our people must realize what an abundance of natural talent lies dormant in them, and how lively is the urge to make use of it. Let us create an opportunity for its development.

In the theatre young people should find everything that is helpful in educating the body to its utmost beauty and expressiveness. In the propitious future men and women physicians who have also been educated in aesthetics will supervise the physical instruction of the young. They will give them advice about diet, exercise, massage, gymnastics, care of the skin and hair. Young people will be taught the technique of the dance from simple acrobatics to the physical interpretation of psychic concepts—that is, to the genuine art of the mime. They will, however, not merely imitate Greek dances. The principles of beauty and of movement that will prevail will be those of our own German race. Sculptors and painters will teach them to understand their bodies and to dress them so that their beauty and expressiveness are heightened. Finally, they will be made familiar with the art of poetry. Any high-school girl can bawl out a slangy song, but scarcely one out of ten thousand can recite a poem, and our professional actors least of all.

From among such young connoisseurs engaging in the mimic art as a recreation, the more talented will quite naturally develop into professional artists, just as in horsemanship certain riders, the so-called masters of the hunt, serve others as examples and instructors.

Not only the dance but every sort of bodily sport is helpful to the actor, especially acrobatics. The Shakespearian fools were by no means the academic bores into which they have been transformed by the dictates of the literati. The Shakespearian fool is the twin brother of the eccentric dancer. In him acrobatics were made serviceable to the drama. This is the only way in which we can attain to a genuine physical culture. Such a culture affects posture, gesture, and speech, and also brings about a general standardization of performance that is indispensable to a successful production.

This knowledge is brought home to us by our insight not only into Greek culture but also into that of the Japanese. The art of Kawakami and Sada Yacco, which we have found so enthralling is incomprehensible unless one considers certain national standards of education for physical and oral expression. The Japanese actor does not shriek and does not rant. There is seldom loud talk upon the stage, and nothing ever happens which would offend the most fastidious company. Yet the Japanese theatre reaches heights of intensity of which we have no idea and does so simply by stylistic means. In whatever is shown upon the stage, whether it be the most tragic circumstance, the most terrible mental anguish, the maddest abandonment, or the most brazen buffoonery, the measured rhythms of the dance are always observed, just as in the field of plastic art the Japanese woodcarver always respects the confines of the plane in which he works.

The Japanese art of acting is indebted for this supremacy of style to its vital connection with fundamental principles, that is, with the elementary physical sources of mimic art. These principles are identical with those of the dance, of acrobatics, of wrestling, and of fencing.

4

We have been unaccustomed to look for and to value in the actor an independent, self-sufficient, and creative artistry. In the dissertations of critics and theorists the actor used to be represented as important only in so far as he was a purveyor of literary values. On this score, however, the general public instinctively felt differently and more correctly than did the literary world. But the decisions of the latter were final. Only the cerebral artist was important. People did not stop to consider that this line of reasoning, carried to its logical conclusion, would make the art of acting nothing but applied psychology and therefore no art at all. As a result, plays and their performers were appreciated only if they furthered some literary objective. The specifically thespian concept was so subordinated that today we can name only isolated actors who are of any importance in contemporary life. These are usually older actors who grew up in an era when these matters were considered in a different light and when, therefore, even in small court theatres one found really great artists.

Furthermore, we suddenly observe with dismay that our most accomplished performers are rapidly dying out and that there are few actors left who can give us, complete in form and individual in conception, an embodiment of the characters created by our great dramatic poets. Such art demands the ability to surrender body and soul entirely to the laws of rhythm. It requires that the actor be informed by the rhythms of the play and, most elemental of all, that the force of natural rhythm in the actor's own body beat unimpeded. In recent years this force was intentionally suppressed in those possessing it. It was uprooted from their natures so that they might be more useful as interpreters of a more literary, more critical, more cerebral, world of ideas.

To grasp the basic techniques of the art of acting abstractly and to present them understandably is difficult. We have, for so long, thought and spoken of acting only from a literary point of view that now we must learn again to judge it artistically, just as we have also had to learn to regard painting pictorially, sculpture plastically, and decoration constructively, according to the particular elements peculiar to each of them. Latin races always accuse us Germans of not being able to do this because it is not in our nature. Where art and the stage were concerned we were supposed to be too intellectually critical, too devoted to the world of ideas, and not naïve enough in the realm of the senses. Goethe, to be sure, gave us a notable picture of the actor's art in *Wilhelm Meister*. But if we are seeking a classic criticism of the art of acting in the artistic sense we must go farther back. Farther even than Lessing's *Dramaturgie*, which is almost entirely literary, to old Georg Christof Lichtenberg, whose letters about Garrick are unsurpassed. He understood the secret of bodily co-ordination in the actor when he wrote of Garrick:

His way of walking, of shrugging his shoulders, of folding his arms, of putting on his hat and sometimes pulling it over his eyes, and sometimes knocking it sidewise off his forehead, doing everything with an easy movement of his limbs as though each were his right hand—this is refreshing to behold. One feels free and strong himself when one sees the strength and sureness in his movements, and notices what control he has over the muscles of his body. One looks serious when he does, wrinkles one's brow when he does, smiles when he smiles. There is a sort of secret happiness about him which is so engaging that one's whole heart goes out to this delightful man.

There are still such actors even today. Only we do not realize it because we are accustomed to pay attention solely to the way in which they embody literature and seldom notice the way in which they create a harmony in the pattern of movement and in the spoken word. Not until they play unliterary roles do we notice something of this. And it is for this reason that we are often more readily aware of acting ability in variety shows or in quite simple sketches and dialogues than in the more lofty literary drama—just as we more readily detect artistic ability in a simple still life than in a more elaborate composition.

An example: When Lili Marberg left Munich, that center of art mourned more than at the departure of many a famous actor who for decades had depicted all the exalted heroes of our classical masterpieces. Lili Marberg had never portrayed one of the monumental feminine figures who stride through the world of our literary culture. She played mostly in plays which were merely the fashion of the moment. Some of them were cleverly constructed; many more were not. None of them were classics. She was neither Ophelia nor Cordelia, Iphigenia nor Lady Macbeth, Klärchen nor Gretchen, Joan nor Judith, nor even one of those dulcet beauties who, looking like Meissen statuettes, skip through the bright measures of Molière's comedies.

And yet, on her departure from that Munich circle in which everyone engages in imaginative and colorful creative activity, it seemed as though a light had been extinguished.

If Marberg played an ingénue, she did not endow the role with the pedantic results of psychological research. She grasped instinctively the rhythmic formula which gave the girl—not yet fully developed but already faintly sex-conscious—her typical appearance and form of expression. She did not grasp it; she allowed herself to be grasped by it. And from the rhythm which pulsed through her being every element of speech and gesture was developed with instinctive logic. Therefore everything about her was in perfect harmony. For this reason we were captivated by her so that we, too, experienced through all our senses this perfect concord.

Because, with her, rhythmical form was basic and elemental, it was developed, in a sense, into the actual rhythms of the dance. This was obvious in her interpretation of Salome. That which was elemental in her bodily rhythm lent her a childish innocence which, like a modest veil, seemed to cover the most provocative gestures of her Salome. Her dance is sacrificial. She must suffer death in order to know love. Her dance is a tragedy.

The scope of such genuine originality in an actor does not matter; it may be broad or narrow; the point is that it is real. Marberg grasps the basic rhythms of every role with that infallibility of unhampered instinct which is only vouchsafed to an original talent. She grasps it not intellectually—that way least of all; she grasps it physically with her body and with her instincts. She becomes in her flesh and blood the incarnation of a rhythm which manifests itself through her whole personality. The tone of her voice, her carriage, the movement of her shoulders, her arms, her hands to the very tips of her fingers, her hips and feet, and even her clothes are controlled by the same rhythm, tuned to a single scale, fashioned in one and the same pattern. It is this that makes the actor into an artist. This alone. The text, the literary subject matter, is vitalized, is expanded into a work of art only after it is physically and rhythmically embodied by the actor, and only when the audience is aroused by it and thus finally convinced of its truth.

Under the domination of the literary theatre one had the opposite idea. The actor as a creative artist was eliminated or at least subordinated as much as possible. He was used merely as a vehicle for the transmission of ideas, as material that, together with other material objects, was to be used to depict literary concepts and poetic moods, to portray social conditions, ethical situations, psychological and moral processes. That under these conditions the highly personal and creative art of acting did not succumb altogether, we have only the actors themselves to thank. Even though they did not all admit it openly, they struggled against these handicaps instinctively and individually.

The time has now come when the results of this situation alarm us. The literary drama that caused these circumstances is exhausted. Everything indicates a fundamental change. Because of the Artists' Theatre, the leading circles of German cultural life are again seriously concerning themselves with the theatre and with the art of acting. They are sure to promote here the same principles that they promulgate with regard to the other arts. In order that they themselves may enjoy more frequently the highest accomplishments of the stage, the cultural leaders of Germany will win for this art the right to develop according to its own intrinsic nature. Here too we must return to tradition and resurrect in the actor's art that most fundamental and essential element—rhythm, in movement, in speech, and in gesture.

IV

Stage and Auditorium

THE Artists' Theatre has a relief stage. It is both amusing and alarming to realize, from the discussions to which this term "relief stage" has given rise, how unaccustomed we are to consider the theatre as a problem in design. Otherwise, the expression "relief stage" would never have been mistaken for a technical term, in the same sense in which we speak of a revolving stage or an elevator stage. Nor would anyone ever have thought of this type of staging as one thinks of a motor or of some other piece of machinery. The expression "relief stage" is not a technical term but a stylistic one. To build a relief stage certain technical construction is, to be sure, necessary—as in the realization of any other artistic concept. But these mechanical devices are not ends in themselves, and it is immaterial whether or not such constructions are exact reproductions of those employed in the Artists' Theatre. It would be theoretically quite possible to achieve the same results,[1] or even more effective ones, by other means.

The purpose of the relief stage is to intensify the dramatic experience. This phenomenon does not occur upon the stage. It occurs in the mind and spirit of the spectator in response to the happenings upon the stage. The spectator is captivated by impressions which reach him through the medium of his senses—through his eye and through his ear. The theatre must, therefore, be so constructed that these optical and acoustical impressions may be communicated to the spectator as directly and forcefully as possible.

To this end, relief has always been the most serviceable artistic form: not only for the eye, but also for the ear. Actually, one does not need a demonstration with regard to sound, because it is obvious that the spoken word, as well as the singing tone, will be sent out into the auditorium more strongly and clearly from a shallow scene, shut in above and at the sides, than from a deep one, because the sound waves do not disperse—backwards, sidewards, and upwards—but are thrown forward in the direction in which they are effective.

Even those who have found nothing else to praise in the Artists' Theatre are amazed at its acoustics. These were further improved by the use of wood paneling throughout the auditorium. Results were obtained which would formerly have been considered impossible. For instance, in the cathedral scene in *Faust*, the Evil Spirit, though hidden, could give the entire text in whispers. A mere breath made every syllable clearly audible even to the farthest seats. It was as though a raging host of demons stormed through the house. Many accents thundered, though spoken in a whisper. The effect was ghostly and supernatural, as though it were the revelation of an experience actually taking place within Gretchen's mind. At the rehearsals we were all surprised by what could be done in these scenes without becoming incomprehensible. The actor playing the Spirit reduced the volume of his whispers to such an extent that in any other theatre, even in the most intimate one, he would have been quite inaudible. And yet it is only by a reduction in volume that one gets the effect the poet desired —a voice which is heard by Gretchen only in her thoughts.

It is a discovery as old as the theatre itself that, as soon as it is necessary to communicate certain important passages, singers and speakers involuntarily press forward so that they assume positions similar to the arrangement of figures in a relief. They do this, if only for the purpose of "making a point," "getting an effect," or "putting over" a popular number. The performer feels instinctively and knows from experience that in this position he is most effective, both because he is less likely to be covered by a fellow player or by a piece of stage property and also because he leaves the background far enough behind him so that it will have less power to attract attention away from him.

The director is continually required to fight against the inclination of the performer to go too far in this instinctive urge to set himself in relief. Against south-European performers the director is helpless. No matter what he does to discourage them, at the height of the action their temperament will sweep them down toward the front of the stage. We have come to consider this swooping forward as absurdly inartistic. Our feeling in the matter, however, has probably been influenced by the fact that previously such forward stage positions brought the performer into the direct illumination of the footlights, which by their inverted position, shining up from below, turned him into a caricature. But has it after all been advantageous to inhibit in the performer such a strong dramatic impulse? Would it not be better to arrange the stage, the proscenium, and the light sources —which all are of secondary importance—to suit the actor's instinctive forward urge and so make available to him his favorite playing space? It would, without question.

This was not done in the past because before the introduction of electric light the footlights were the chief source of illumination, and it was necessary for them to be adjusted and cared for. But now, since we have electric light with which we are able to illuminate whatever part of the stage is most useful to us, it would be foolish to cling to arrangements which are obsolete. If from dramatic necessity the performance develops into a sort of relieflike arrangement, sources of light should be installed in that part of the stage toward which the performers repeatedly experience this compulsion. Actors should not be allowed to appear at a disadvantage in that particular part of the stage where for dramatic, acoustic, and visual reasons they are most effective.

And so in the Artists' Theatre by the arrangement of rows of lights in the architrave of the foreproscenium and in the moveable overhead bridges of the inner proscenium, the performers and the groupings at the front of the stage receive direct illumination from above. The small footlights fulfill in general only the auxiliary function that in natural lighting is contributed by reflection from the ground; that is, the eradication of unpleasant shadows from the face. On occasion stronger lights were supplied so that a player who was crouching or lying on the ground might be more clearly distinguished (for example, Gretchen in the dungeon scene). In general it may be said that in the front part of the stage, and particularly in the proscenium area, every possibility of controlling light sources should be utilized; for, since every drama in its decisive moments pushes forward away from the background, one must be prepared for a multiplicity of situations in the foreground and be adept at supplying suitable lighting for each.

2

It was, therefore, no superficial straining after effectiveness or picturesqueness which brought the relief stage into being. It was, on the contrary, designed according to the dictates of the drama and conditioned by its own activities. The relief stage got its name from the fact that the impression it creates is that of a relief. This effect, however, is arrived at not by arbitrarily imposing a principle of plastic art upon a dramatic performance after the manner of "living pictures," but by letting the drama develop according to its own necessities; by putting nothing—absolutely nothing—in its way; and by simply allowing the drama to create its own surroundings as a snail builds its house.

Furthermore, since it is in the consciousness of the spectator that the dramatic experience finally becomes a reality, the drama must also create the auditorium. The physical rhythms of the play are transformed at the curtain line into the emotional vibrations which move the audience. Therefore the proscenium, which is the dividing line between stage and auditorium, is the most important architectural feature in the theatre. It defines the space within which, by a certain alchemy, a conglomeration of people, objects, sounds, tones, lights, and shadows are arranged so as to create an intellectual and emotional harmony. On the stage itself this harmony, this work of art, does not exist. Nothing of what the spectator experiences is behind the footlights. Anyone knows this who has ever stood in the wings during a performance, or who has ever acted himself. To be sure, the person who watches from the wings, and even the actor upon the stage, may receive a strong emotional impact, but it is of quite a different sort from that which the audience is receiving at exactly the same moment. For only in the audience may one observe the amalgamation of many abstract perceptions into a single harmonious experience.

But if, from the standpoint of the spectator, we separate this total effect into the smallest fractions of time which may be differentiated in the progress of the whole, if we separate the moving drama as the moving picture film separates the progress of action into very small units —or "frames," as they are called—we receive each time a visual impression of a picture in the form of a relief. And this is true not only of the relief stage of the Artists' Theatre but also of every other stage. On a deep stage, however, the pictures in these frames are much less vivid and well composed, because here the composition of a stage picture in the form of a relief is much more difficult, first, because the background is too restless, and second, because the physical presence of the performer is impaired by the many supplementary objects which a deep stage of the conventional sort needs to set a scene at all —especially if the stage picture is supposed to represent a scene from real life.

These brief pictures, these frames, these momentary groupings in the form of a relief, do not arise from conscious arrangement. They are not poses or stills in a pictorial sense. They develop of themselves from the dramatic necessities of the play. Every dramatic action consists of a series of important moments, and the actors who are concerned with these points of climax must of necessity function in approximately the same plane. The more the actors work in one plane, the more strongly their action will hang together. This is important. For no matter how deep a stage may be, the actors, and particularly the director, will feel (sometimes instinctively and sometimes consciously) that the performers who at the moment carry the major part of the action, who "have a scene together," should appear as far as possible in one plane. Otherwise, the action falls apart and finally becomes unintelligible.

At the rehearsals of any theatre you may choose, with the exception of those that bungle the whole business completely, one may find the director laboring day after day to bring those performers who are working together in a certain situation into the same plane. Scenery is rebuilt, furniture and properties dragged about, an exit introduced, the text condensed, or a pantomime interpolated. All this feverish activity for the purpose of arranging a scene so that those actors who, at a given moment, belong together may occupy approximately the same working space. And how the poor director must struggle if the depth of his stage presents insurmountable difficulties! If, for example, a performer appears in the background on an elevation—a rock or a balcony—and from that position must enter into a scene with the other principal actors who are stationed downstage below him, what building and constructing and arranging must go on merely to give the impression that two widely separated groups are approximately in one plane!

To be sure, the average director does not so torment himself because his taste has been refined by a study of the noblest works of art. (He often has no taste at all.) Nor does he do so because he may have read Hildebrand's book on *The Problem of Form*. (He has never heard of Hildebrand.) He goes to all this trouble because his practical experience has taught him that unless he does so the situation will be ineffective or will not be understood. Whatever the drama may be, the effort is always to impress the eye by a series of reliefs. It is not the farthest plane of a relief (the background) which should serve as the principal plane but the nearest one, "the one in which the highest figures meet," says Hildebrand in his chapter on the design of the relief. In the drama too, it is the highest figures, that is, those that are farthest forward, which are most important. These are forced by the action of the drama itself into the plane that is nearest the front, and in order to be dramatically effective, they require a background running parallel to them. Goethe was the first to recognize and comment on the fact that the progress of dramatic treatment is shown in a succession of bas-reliefs, each one portraying a moment of action.

This seems to be contradicted by the way many dramatists, and among them certain important literary dramatists, expressly describe the stage sets to be used in their plays. Not infrequently they demand the meticulous reproduction of an historical background or of some modern place. To set such a stage, a multitude of petty properties is indispensable, and in a scene conceived in the form of a relief, these are not easily accommodated. Such a stage must have depth, which almost destroys the effect of the relief. But the contradiction is more apparent than real. One becomes convinced of this if on a well-ordered stage one watches the performance of such a literary piece as, let us say, one of the later works of Ibsen. The meticulous reproduction of a specific environment, which is revealed to the spectator at the rise of the curtain, exists for his eye and for his consciousness only so long as the action itself has not yet taken possession of him. From the moment when he is carried away by the acting, that detailed illustrative setting disappears from his consciousness, and if in the further course of the play it ever bobs up again, it is either to annoy him or to indicate to him that the performance has begun to drag.

For the greater part of the dramatic action, this reproduction of a particular place, together with its necessary depth of stage, is at best superfluous and at worst annoying. The spectator must continually shake off the distraction it imposes so that he may direct his attention to those things which are really important. Since this is so, why not spare him the pains and choose in the beginning a form of design which will prove more satisfactory to him, as well as to the actor and the author? In other words, a design in relief!

But there are some who will protest: It can't be done —for what then will become of the mood of the play, of the "atmosphere" which the playwright has so lovingly described and through which he brings home to our sensibilities the emotional content of his piece? To this one can only reply that if the author needs so much visual aid to carry the import of his play, he is certainly a dilettante dramatist, though he may be an admirable literary person outside the theatre. If he does not need it, this detailed reproduction of an environment does exactly the opposite of what he wants it to do. It directs our attention away from the essential nature of his work, and one does him no service in giving it to him.

3

Let us now watch the actor. He too retains his relationship to the details of the scenery only so long as he is not in action. Shortly after the beginning of the play it becomes his duty—by stern command of the director —to identify himself with the surrounding objects of this carefully built-up background. But as soon as he gets into his part, as soon as he begins to act, the background no longer exists for him. The principal group always pushes forward into one plane. The director is, of course, a "penetrating psychologist" who "understands" the author to the effect that the performer must, now and then, resume his relationship to the environment. Occasionally, therefore, he issues such a decree and the actor, with the appropriate catchwords supplied for that purpose, detaches himself from the plane in which the action is taking place. He goes upstage, throws a log on the fire, lights the customary cigarette, looks out of the window, and then, as soon as he has something to do in the real action, returns quickly into the plane of the main group. There is not a theatre in the world in which this shift of relationship between the actor and the environment is accomplished in such a way that one does not notice the device and feel annoyed by it. It is and always will be a dilettante contrivance, an irrelevant by-product of the novel to which the authentic, the un-literary, dramatist never stoops. It is untheatrical.

We expect the theatre to be theatrical and want it to be so; anything that is out of harmony with sound the-atrical design we consider inartistic. Since it is impossible to resist for more than a few minutes the urge of the dramatic action toward a relief effect in the foremost plane, the result is that the stage remains unused for al-most two thirds of its depth. So it is necessary to fill it up with a quantity of illustrative detail which makes the background even more obtrusive. Such a background in turn distracts attention from the performers and from the dramatic action.

But mob scenes! How can one accommodate crowds if one has no depth? Let us ask in return: With what number does the conception of a crowd begin? With eleven, seventeen, thirty-nine, seven hundred? The num-ber is immaterial. A crowd is on the stage if the effect of a crowd reaches the eyes and ears of the audience. The conventional theatre with its tiers of boxes needs, to be sure, a good many people and, therefore, requires a deeper stage. For, from the higher rows with their broad view over the scene, one may count the heads upon the stage. Also the bad design of the proscenium makes many voices necessary in order to send the sound of a great crowd through the entire house. Here one must work with quantity. But a relieflike arrangement makes it possible to get the effect of a crowd by quality and by valid artistic analogy. Moreover, the amphitheatre, which is a continuation of the stage and is a form indigenous to the drama, allows no such view over the heads of the actors. The eye is not encouraged to probe the depths of the scene and to compute whether or not there are actually as many examples of homo sapiens accommodated there as are required to constitute a crowd.

On the contrary, only a thin row of figures is necessary in front of a shallow background which shuts off the rest of the stage. By certain artistic devices such a scene may be made to seem filled with people. Hodler, in his famous fresco, *The Retreat from Marignano*, gives the impression of the passing of an army by twelve full figures and about as many parts of figures which with their heads, limbs, and weapons fill up the chinks left by the full figures. And the impression that this army is retreating and must defend itself from the pursuing enemy is achieved by having the last man—one single figure!—separated from the main group by about the width of a man and turned back with uplifted sword. This simple device is as old as the prehistoric beginnings of culture. Actually, the bas-reliefs of the Stone Age which have been found near Thaingen represent a higher cultural level than do the most elaborate scenic pictures of the modern stage. The development of the theatre would be quite simple and straightforward if no one expected anything of the drama except what is dramatic and theatrical.

Unfortunately, our theatre has taken on many other aspects. It has been used for the dissemination of literature, and there are educated people who believe it should be used for nothing else. It has been used for sensationalism—and what many of our large metropolitan playhouses put upon their stages is something quite different from the art of the theatre. They must pander to the animal appetites, and their mammoth productions are not concerned with dramatic art, even when the work of a great dramatic poet is used as a pretext for catering to sensationmongers. Also our theatres are used for opera, and in opera it is comparatively immaterial whether or not the scene design is organically related to the drama. In opera, neither the tremendous size of the settings nor the opulence of the appointments is distracting, for the opera, as well as the music drama, projects both the person of the actor and the entire dramatic action into the realm of the colossal. This is brought about by the orchestra and the voices of the performers, which are so much more powerful in singing than in speaking. The devices of opera are too forceful for a stage that is to be used for the spoken drama. From its beginning opera was intended for the festival halls of palaces.

Opera is quite at home on the deep stage and in the balconied theatre, both of which were built for it and developed with it. If four trombones are not sufficient, then eight will do it. And if thirty choristers do not roar loudly enough, in Heaven's name give us a hundred! In opera, everything depends on the music. But more of this in the chapter about opera.

4

The Artists' Theatre is not another type of stage reform. The reformers, led by certain prominent theatre men, took the existing circumstances of construction and design as they are to be found in our conventional theatre and concentrated their efforts on creating a heightened effect for the drama and the performer. They did this by means of certain alterations and simplifications—as an illustration, consider the so-called "Shakespearian stage" —or by ingenious inventions that made possible a more rapid handling of stage machinery. The revolving stage and the shift of scene without a curtain are examples of such reforms. At other times they merely attempted to create more tasteful stage pictures. We are indebted to these reformers for a multitude of ideas and experiences, but their greatest contribution lies in the proof which their work affords that attempts to reform the conventional theatre are useless.

Theatre reform merely aims at a purification of the existing ineptitudes and improprieties. The Artists' Theatre plans to rebuild the stage from the ground up. It is not just a matter of the stage and what is on the stage. Instead, the entire problem of design as it touches the drama and the spectators should be considered, both on the stage and in the auditorium. The theatre is an organic whole.

The essential idea of the Artists' Theatre is accordingly not to be found in technical novelties, mechanical inventions, tricks, and apparatus. On the contrary, the only important technical elements are in the architectural solutions by means of which plastic art may create, for the drama and for the performer, the most effective frame, and for the spectator, the most favorable conditions of receptivity.

It follows, then, that by a wholesale simplification which others have tried (such as playing in front of Gobelin tapestries) [2] nothing important is accomplished. The problem is to evolve a stage from the basic principles of dramatic art, from the stage to develop an auditorium which is closely related to it, and then to unite these two related areas (along with the necessary auxiliary facilities) in an appropriate building. Thus the construction of a theatre is elevated to the position of an architectural project. Max Littmann, the builder of The Artists' Theatre, has explained in a monograph the steps he took to accomplish this enterprise. I need only say here that, except for minor details occasioned by certain features of the site and by the relatively limited funds available, he did not need to deviate from the plan which I worked out with him and which I published along with his sketches in my book, *The Stage of the Future*.

If a more extensive piece of land and a larger endowment had been at our disposal, it would have been easy to build a working space more in accordance with the original plan, especially to give more depth to the stage and to the storerooms. This added area would not have been used to deepen the playing space, which was sufficient even for mob scenes. Its purpose would have been to make the most of the light sources in order that the background might be illuminated more intensively. Light has the power to dissolve a physical object, to dematerialize it, so that an intensively illuminated expanse of canvas changes for the eye of the spectator into an illusion

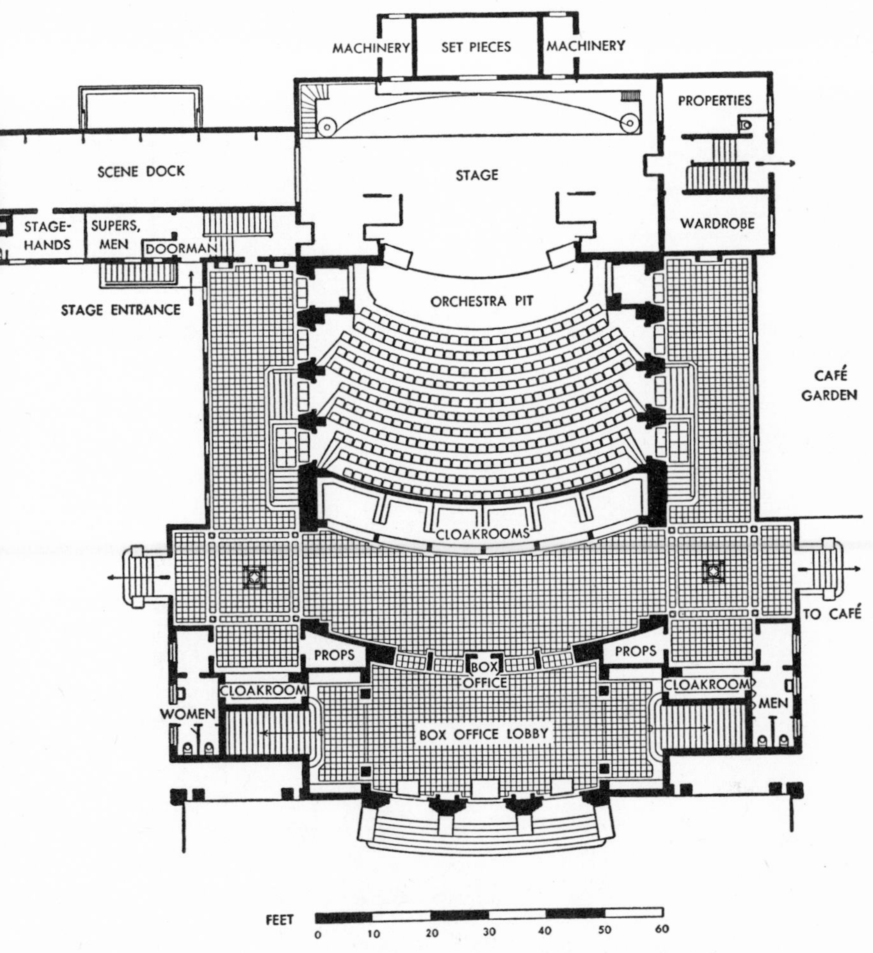

Fig. 1. Plans for the ground floor (*Erdgeschoss*) of the Munich Artists' Theatre as drawn by its architect, Max Littmann. Reproduced with English legends from his book, *Das Münchner Künstlertheater* (Munich: L. Werner, 1908).

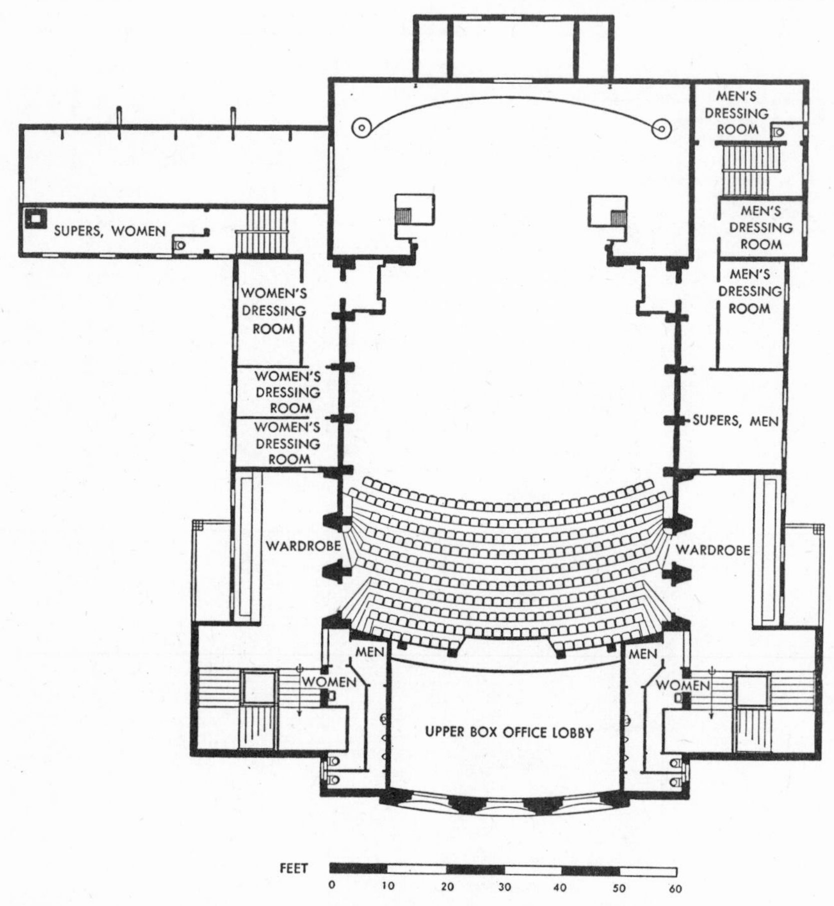

Fig. 2. Plans for the second story (*Halbgeschoss*) of the Munich Artists' Theatre as drawn by its architect, Max Littmann. Reproduced with English legends from his book, *Das Münchner Künstlertheater* (Munich: L. Werner, 1908).

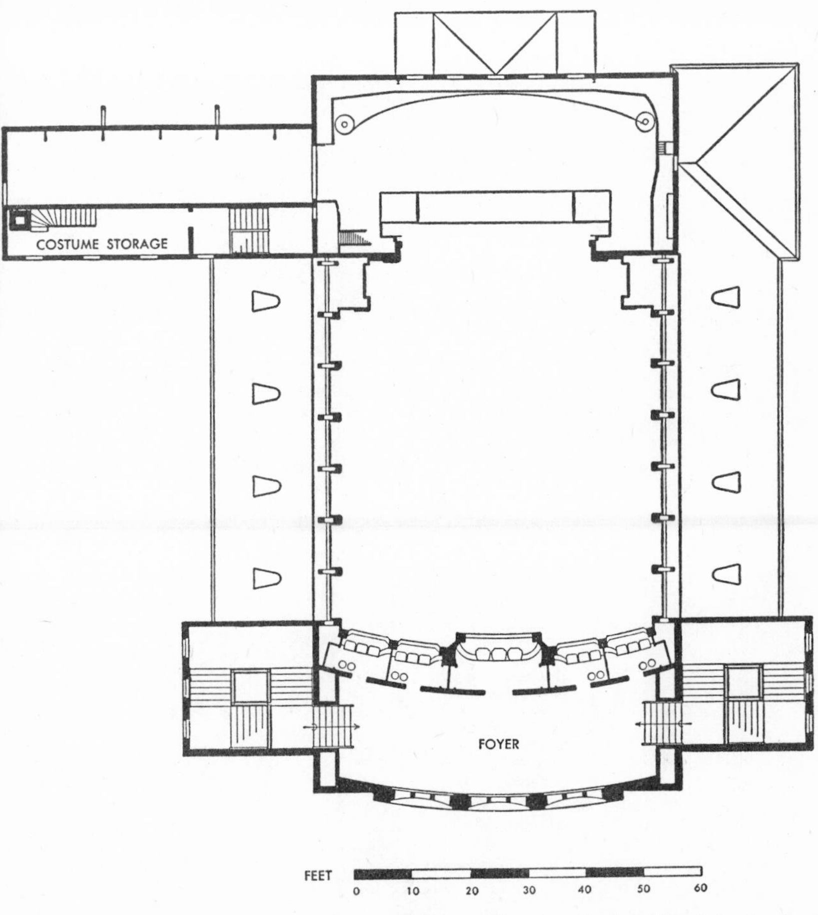

Fig. 3. Plans for the top story (*Obergeschoss*) of the Munich Artists' Theatre as drawn by its architect, Max Littmann. Reproduced with English legends from his book, *Das Münchner Künstlertheater* (Munich: L. Werner, 1908).

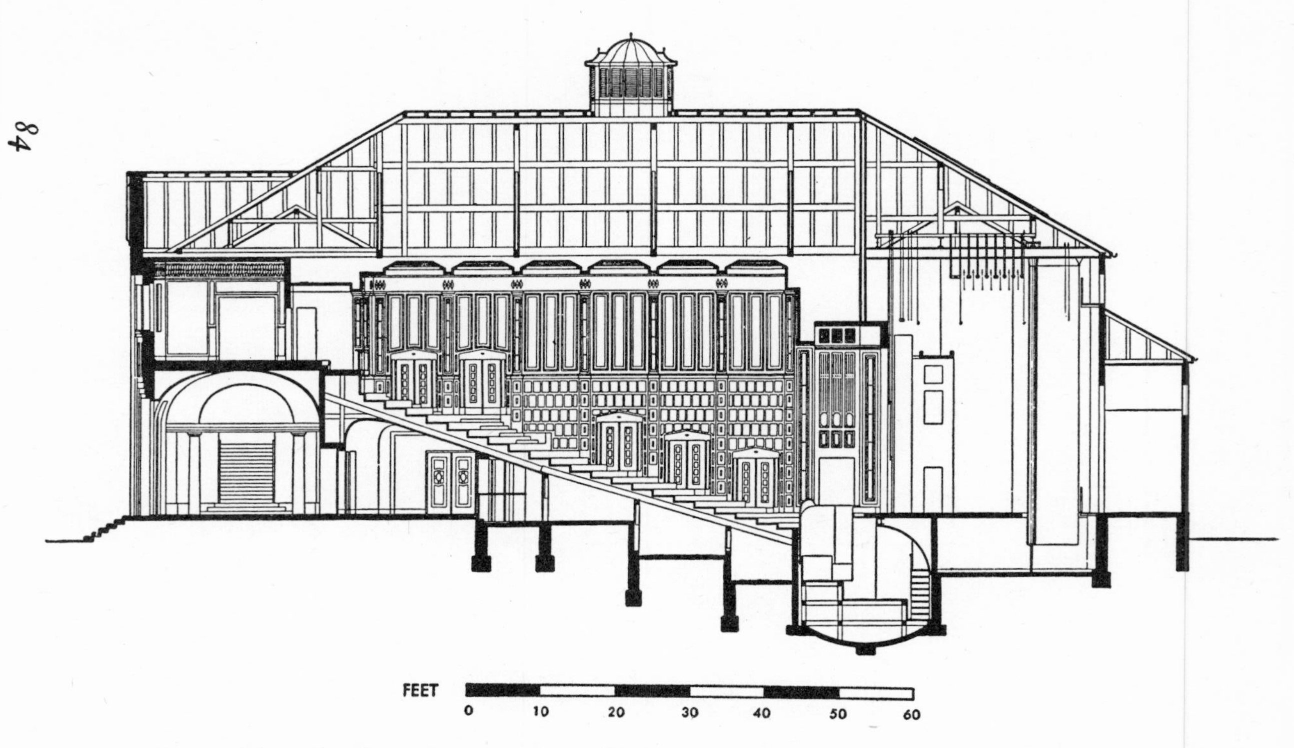

Fig. 4. Plans showing a cross section (*Längenschnitt*) of the Munich Artists' Theatre as drawn by its architect, Max Littmann. Reproduced with English legends from his book, *Das Münchner Künstlertheater* (Munich: L. Werner, 1908).

of infinite space. For this, however, one needs not only a certain strength of light, but also a certain distance between this highly intensified body of light and the illuminated plane, so that the vitalizing quality of the illumination may have full effect. In the Artists' Theatre, light sources in the upper and, more particularly, in the lower part of the set pieces on the sunken portion at the back of the stage cannot, in our opinion, quite do justice to this function because we were not allowed to move the back wall of the stage out several meters into the park.

There will need to be many improvements in this respect, for this is a question of great importance. Light is, and will continue to be, the most important factor in the development of stage design. Modern electrical technique offers possibilities which it would be folly to disregard. To use them correctly, to distribute and regulate these immense and manifold masses of light with artistic effect, requires the creative spirit of a sculptor. If on the stage an accurate perception of artistic values is considered necessary with regard to wigs, costumes, draperies, and the like, how much more must this be the case with regard to light, which governs the appearance and value of all such things, including the performers themselves! Engineers and electricians who have so much to contribute may no longer be ignored. Workers in the plastic arts must recognize and welcome them. What the result of such cooperation can be was demonstrated by the lighting effects achieved in the very first season at the Artists' Theatre.

In the Artists' Theatre the forestage and the middle stage receive their light from a forward overhead position. The inner stage has its own, independent sources of light.

These are arranged so as to produce all shades of light. All possible atmospheric moods are created by the light itself in such a way as to satisfy the most exacting aesthetic standards. This lighting apparatus (which is provided with five colors) can indicate not only color values but also all gradations of light and dark. And, by changes in the size of the proscenium opening, both broad expanses and quite intimate arrangements of space may be suggested. Formerly, for example, the director had no other means of suggesting the idea of a room than by the erection of a room set, with a collection of furniture, which of course takes much too long. Now the creative ability of the designer comes to the director's aid, and by shrinking the proscenium opening and lowering the lights, he creates the *impression* of an interior—not the interior itself but merely such relations of light and mass as are required to awaken in the imagination of the spectator the conception of a certain space such as the poet suggests in a particular scene. An accomplishment of such significance demands unusual imaginative and creative ability—this will be admitted even by the most crabbed critics of every improvement in our theatre.

The co-operation of experts in the plastic arts is not new in the theatre. Leonardo often busied himself with problems of the stage. Raphael painted the decorations for Ariosto's *Suppositi*—we know indeed that these were composed in the relieflike, simplified style of the Pompeian frescos. In the Renaissance and in the baroque, rococo, and classic periods the arrangements of the theatre and of the scenery were put into the hands of architects and painters (for example, Palladio's Teatro Olympico at Vicenza). Goethe hunted zealously for painters. Italians from the famous school of Galli Bibiena and artists like Fuentes, as well as German painters, were considered, but he did not find what he sought among any of them. Still, Schinkel accomplished something in that in his plans he placed the plastic arts at the service of the architectural designer, and he proposed a type of illumination which was especially suited to meet the needs of the stage. Hoffmann and Blechen also exerted themselves in this direction, and Immermann had the decorations for his Shakespeare stage at Düsseldorf made by Schadow and his pupils.

The conventional theatres of our day have had need of the painter. However, they have never allowed either the painter or the architect to practice his art free from all restrictions save those imposed by the function of the drama. They have forced artists to renounce the laws of art and bow instead to the laws of mechanics. Within these restrictions—as we have shown—even the greatest pictorial skill could not provide an artistic effect. So that, instead of supporting the drama and the performer and enhancing them, plastic art impeded rather than advanced dramatic expression. But what the designer and painter can do for the stage may easily be seen in every individual case in which they have had a free hand. They invariably put on productions which are delightful and inspiring, and in which the plastic arts are always important and, indeed, may be the determining factor in the style of the whole.

Max Reinhardt has done a lasting service in bringing plastic art to the fore and proving, through some of its best representatives, that it possesses the power to free the basic elements of dramatic masterpieces from absolete mannerisms of production and to make them acceptable to the public and in harmony with the best standards of taste. This is important. Plastic art should not be added to dramatic art merely to make a superficial effect. Every artistic solution of a theatre problem should lead to a drastic reduction of scenic paraphanalia and make use of the minimum of representational imagery.

The Artists' Theatre, therefore, has a stage arrangement which does not merely allow for the occasional performance of a piece according to this fashion, but which recognizes these principles once and for all and raises them to the commanding position they deserve. Moreover, the architect Max Littmann, the painters Benno Becker and Fritz Erler, as well as the sculptor Adolf von Hildebrand have co-operated in distinguished fashion in the technical solution of the stage problems. The principles of design which Hildebrand set forth in his discussion of *The Problem of Form* were organically developed out of the nature of the drama.

The plan is, in itself, quite simple. The technical part of it was designed by the mechanical director of the Munich Court Theatre, Julius Victor Klein. The basic idea was derived from the original ideas of the artists who developed the theatre.

In front of the stage is an orchestra pit. When this is not in use it is covered over. A wide girdle of footlights affords the eye a satisfying transition into that realm behind them, a realm which is governed by other special laws than those which obtain for the spectator before the house lights are lowered. The whole stage plan is shallow in relation to its width. We want neither a peep show nor a panorama, but rather that design which is most favorable to moving bodies, which unites them in a rhythmic pattern and which at the same time throws the sound waves out into the house. The objective is not the painting with depth of perspective but the flat relief. By purely architectural means we created three planes: a forestage, or proscenium; a middle stage, which is usually used as the playing space; and an inner stage.

The gatelike architecture of the proscenium is repeated on the middle stage in the so-called "inner proscenium," the towerlike terminations of which at either side prevent the audience from looking beyond the limits of the stage sidewise into the workroom. They also make wings and borders unnecessary because they are joined together above by a roof—as Schinkel once proposed. Their neutral arrangement with doors and windows makes them available now as part of the proscenium and now as part of the stage. They fulfill their function as an inner proscenium particularly when the second curtain, in front of the back part of the stage, is in use. The bridgelike roof which joins the "towers" may be placed at different heights and the stage opening thus made smaller by a similar use of the side pieces.

Moreover, the level of the back part of the stage may be raised or lowered either in part or as a whole. If the back of the scene represents an expanse of landscape, the back part of the stage is sunk so deeply that the floor is no longer visible to the spectator.

If the figure of the actor now appears on the stage, the spectator unconsciously assumes that the intervening space which he, the spectator, cannot see, is really as great as it would have to be in order to make the human figure appear in relation to the distant landscape as it actually appears to the eye. Therefore, the relationship between the actor and the background is always right, since it is established in the eye of the beholder. On the conventional peep-show stage this is impossible, since on longer inspection the eye can always compute the actual distance by such fixed measurements as the space between the wings, the boards in the floor, and so on.

On the peep-show stage—as in every panorama or cyclorama—the eye is tricked and cheated. In order to get the effect of space and distance our stage, like every work of art, takes into account the creative power of the eye.

5

The drama is irresistible rhythmic movement. All contributions to dramatic form such as we have been considering here individually and independently must for the sake of the performance as a whole be subject to the laws of this rhythmic movement. If for the sake of elucidation we sometimes cite examples from the field of plastic art, we do so with the understanding that the fundamental principles of the drama are essentially independent.

As in plastic art, so here, the Japanese can offer us fruitful and stimulating examples. Their stage never departs from the authenticity of its dramatic style and never forgets that the drama is rhythmic movement of the body in space. In its artistic development of acrobatics, dancing, pantomime, costume, and decoration it has reached the very highest excellence. It may serve us especially as an example of the harmonious use of color. In the arrangement of his scene, the Japanese director portrays the emotional progress of the piece in a truly remarkable fashion. For example, we have a scene in which a man and a woman are conversing quietly. Suddenly the conversation takes an ominous turn. In an instant, the color harmony is changed. If at first the scene was pale green with a decoration of cherry blossoms, at the significant moment the garments of the characters suddenly fall back from their shoulders revealing undergarments of crimson, and simultaneously several scarlet-clad supernumeraries appear in the background bringing some necessary appurtenance—an altar, a rug—and the color harmony is suddenly blood red and black. The effect is more weird, more horrifying, than all the mechanical thunder and lightning which in our theatre, even in the most naturalistic pieces, make their appearance with such suspicious promptness.

The setting of the Japanese theatre of the best period was kept strictly neutral. It harmonized, to be sure, in a general way with the emotional content of the scene, with the lines of the groupings, and with the costumes. It was, when considered by itself, beautiful in line, form, and color. But in itself it was expressionless, just as the accompanying music was expressionless—rhythmic, monotonous, nothing in itself—yet as an element in the moving spectacle of the whole, highly important, even indispensable.

It cannot be too forcefully repeated that everything except the circumstances of the play, everything except the drama, everything except the actual bodily movement and the rhythm of speech is secondary. No secondary element should be allowed to have any independent significance. Everything should serve to strengthen the dramatic form. This is true of the entire theatre building as well as of the particular setting of single scenes. Especially is it true of the rhythmic play and counterplay of line. The aim here is to connect in significant relationship the vertical lines of the human figure and the predominantly horizontal lines in the painted background, or to emphasize reclining objects by means of lines parallel to the horizontal lines of the stage picture. Add to this the inexhaustible possibilities of color as shown in the handling of colorful draperies against a background, to say nothing of the patterns which the movement of groups and masses brings about against a stationary setting.

Concerning the techniques of painting in perspective, only a few brief references to fundamental principles can be made in this short summary. Let it be clearly understood that here too every inclination toward naturalistic illusion and an effect of depth is avoided. Artistic success can be achieved here only by a strictly architectural handling of planes. One may—to take an example from mural painting—remember how Puvis de Chavannes handles landscapes and architecture, how Feuerbach uses the blue expanse of the sea as a basic element of design in his Medea and Iphigenia pictures, how Marées sets up trees and columns as dynamic verticals against the horizontal planes of earth and clouds, how Tiepolo by elaborate arrangements of significant elements in architecture and landscape conjures up rich surroundings for his groups of figures. Our Munich artists were so successful with style and with design that one realized immediately what a tremendous wealth of creative power was here at our disposal.

6

No one should suppose that this concession to painting contradicts the principle that in the creation of our scenes only genuine material is used. In the sense of stage appearances everything is genuine which gives the proper artistic effect, everything which the eye infers and accepts. But on the stage a copy of an actual object is not genuine in this sense if it prevents the spectator from imagining the scene and the properties. Instead of such a genuine imaginative concept, the conventional theatre is wont to substitute an exact reproduction of reality which some employee has bought ready-made in a wholesale theatrical outfitting shop. Actually a painted wooden sword can give a more genuine effect on the stage than a real one or one that has been carefully copied from the original. Painting itself is genuine material if it is used as such in the sense in which it was used by the old masters.

The conventional theatres, to be sure, also use painting and sometimes do so with amazing skill, but they do not use it according to the laws inherent in painting itself. They use it to accomplish a deception. The plane, which is the fundamental principle of pictorial creation, must, they say, be done away with, and in its place a three-dimensional reality must be mirrored. No greater insult to all fundamental ideas of painting and pictorial effect could be conceived. The Artists' Theatre has brought painting back into good repute upon the stage as a genuine art which brings to life plane surfaces with line and color. Indeed, in the composition of the scene, painting often performs the supremely important task of shutting off the background in an impressively simple way, really shutting it off by a flat surface, a surface entirely in keeping with architectural forms and still in a flat plane. Paintings on the side walls are unnecessary.

It is also superfluous to have the boundary lines of the

stage defined by painting, for this is accomplished by the frame of the outer proscenium of the stage itself in conjunction with the bridgelike roof between the towers of the inner proscenium. Within these towers may be incorporated as part of the indigenous design the pictorial decoration which, as a painted scene in the background, creates the illusion of space and depth. Hildebrand says:

> If we consider what an infinitely different thing a picture is from what it represents in nature, the power which it possesses to create an illusion in mankind would remain a riddle if the picture did not, like nature itself, beget in us the conception of space. Therefore the parallel between nature and art is not to be found in the actual appearance, but in the fact that art and nature possess a similar power of arousing the conception of space. It is not a matter of trickery, by which one is supposed to mistake the picture for a piece of reality as with a panorama, but rather it is a question of the strength of the impressions which are united in the picture.

The peep-show stage of the conventional theatre grew precisely out of this circumstance, that the vulgar concept of the panorama was grafted onto the original and stylized wing-stage technique of the baroque court theatres. Let us hear what Hildebrand has to say on this subject:

> The panorama which gets its effect partly by painting alone, that is, by flat surfaces, and partly by real spatial perspective and plastic representation, tries in this way to transport the spectator into reality so that by an actual deepening of space different visual accommodations will be demanded, as in nature. At the same time it tries to trick us about these actual distances. By means of painting it gives them entirely different meanings. The crude part of this arrangement lies in the fact that, to the sensitive eye, this sort of accommodation is contra-

dicted by the clearness with which one can see at a distance. According to the actual accommodation one is seeing at a distance of a meter, but according to the visual accommodation one is seeing at the distance of a mile. This contradiction is a kind of fraud, and is most uncomfortable.

Every theatregoer is familiar with this fraud because he sees it whenever the curtain goes up on such a panoramic stage. It always takes some time for us to get our bearings in this sham world—or rather, to shake ourselves psychologically free of it. Hildebrand's denunciation falls with devastating fury on all the customary stage practices.

The feeling of reality which the panorama is intended to arouse presupposes an extraordinary obtuseness and crudity of perception. The old-fashioned panorama which is merely a continuous picture is a simple pleasure without dissimulation, intended for children. But the present-day elaborate ones make a perverse appeal to the senses and engender a false feeling of reality in exactly the same way as do displays of wax works.

This era of theatrical culture, together with its literature, belongs in the same world with stone building ornaments made of zinc and painted iron animals in the gardens of the pretentious.

There is one consideration which may occur to certain people. This is the matter of presenting plausibly on the new stage such supernatural figures as ghosts, spirits, and gods. We are so accustomed to degenerate theatricalism with its fake lighting tricks that we have come to expect such representations of superhuman beings to appear before us like the spooks in backstairs romances. As a matter of fact, it is in just such instances that we are able to appreciate what injury the conventional theatre has done us. For example: In the first act of Shakespeare's tragedy we meet the great Julius Caesar wearing his faded earthly trappings. He is aging, ailing, weak; his whole appearance is only a miserable shadow of his majestic self. In the fourth act, however, Caesar's ghost appears. Caesar's ghost! What abysmal vulgarity it takes to represent the ghost of Caesar as a spectre from a silly nursery tale, wrapped in a sheet smeared with red paint and lighted by a spotlight! How infamous to make him a disgusting scarecrow intended to raise goose flesh on servant girls. Caesar's ghost! Could the greatest artist invent a picture too sublime to serve as the apparition of "transfigured Caesar"? Shakespeare left us no doubt concerning the way in which he imagined the apparition. Caesar speaks of himself as an "angel." And Brutus asks, "Art thou a god?" It is important that Brutus realize how he has robbed the world in stabbing Caesar—robbed it of its most majestic human being. Here the spirit of Caesar should take superhuman shape, in shining garments supported by clouds of light.

And so, too, at Macbeth's board, it is not the bloody, dun-colored ass who seats himself. For what have the transfigured in common with the corpse from which it is their triumph to have parted? It is Banquo, the hero, the sanctified, who wears his wounds as blessed martyrs carry the stigmata, as evidences of their resurrection.

Is it any wonder that today people of culture refuse to see the classics as they are presented in the theatre? Too great a disparity exists between such presentations and the conception that is awakened in one's mind simply by reading these masterpieces. With the advent of the new stage, however, cultivated people may be expected to return to the theatre for the performance of these great plays. For here, at long last, they may again find classic drama, unaltered and unmutilated!

7

There is another thing to be considered: The complicated machinery of the conventional theatre demands extended intermissions, not only between the acts but even between the scenes. These halts in the dramatic action are required for the manipulation of elaborate naturalistic settings—even such settings as feature historical accuracy are fundamentally merely banal naturalism. But all such interruptions disrupt the rhythmic structure of a great drama so that it is weakened and sometimes no longer comprehensible. Even the best of today's performances make it difficult to realize that a tragedy by Shakespeare is in itself a complete and balanced structure. The Munich Shakespeare Stage, with its revolving stage floor, was created as a result of the recognition of this important fact. But it was only a half measure and therefore soon succumbed to the prevailing artistic vulgarity. It is easy to understand why, since the decay of an older, sounder culture, scarcely a poet has succeeded in bringing forth a drama of firm and balanced structure. The modern theatre with its wing contraptions and its stage machines has been too discouraging. And yet one may safely wager that such dramas will again appear and be successful when there is a stage on which they can be properly produced.

By the simplification of apparatus and the consequent quick changes, the Artists' Theatre preserved the rhythmic and dramatic structure of the plays that were presented in a fashion which far surpassed all expectations. This was what brought such large audiences again and again into the Artists' Theatre to see the presentation of *Faust*. Here at last the mighty rhythms, the poetic harmonies, appeared in complete and comprehensible unity. If here or there some detail fell short of perfection, it did not matter. The production was a unit and was not disrupted by endless waits for shifts of scene. Voices and figures were not lost in the unfathomable depths of an opera stage designed for ballet fairies and chorus mobs. They emerged from the relief which was a living pattern so plastic and so effective that even foreigners who knew no word of German assured us that they received a definite aesthetic satisfaction. It gave them particular pleasure to watch the way in which the dialogue flew back and forth between the figures arranged against a flat surface, like the expressive hand of a pianist gliding over the keys. The relief stage always emphasized the whole and would not tolerate such ineptitudes as resulted from the naturalism of the deep stage where the organic groupings are dissolved and where the performer is overwhelmed by an arrangement of furniture of the most provincial tastelessness, a stage which forces the actor to indulge in exaggerated grimaces in order to project any important pantomime above the detail of the overburdened background.

At the Artists' Theatre the neutral inner proscenium was not even noticed. The eye slid over it, taking it for granted, so that it made no further impression on the consciousness. The eye was immediately taken up with the performer and the rhythmic sequence of events. The naïve spectator who had not previously "read a bit about it" noticed very little that seemed new or strange to him, for no obstacles were placed in the way of his contact with the only thing that interested him, the performer and the dramatic performance. Everything was so arranged as to give him only such elements as he needed to create for himself the appropriate locale for the happenings which were taking place upon the stage.

8

It would be difficult to find a person so naïve as really to believe in a naturalistic art of scene design, or one who would consider it possible to build a scene that is actually true to nature. Compared to nature, all scenes are quite untrue, impossible, and silly, no matter how carefully and exactly they may be copied from existing locales; yes, even if they are put together from "original" pieces. For the actuality is a stage set, and one must let it go at that. The heritage of the peep show can never be quite denied. And it is well that this is so, for in this fact there is a compulsion toward unreality. That is, toward style.

No theatrical piece, no matter how naturalistic, can possibly be acted on the stage as it happens in real life. Every author must make departures from the rhythms of reality. He must concentrate his material, must leave out irrelevant parts, must emphasize what is characteristic and suppress what does not characterize. It is by the manner in which he deals with his material that he shows whether he is a creative poet, a playwright of a more literary sort, or merely a theatrical confectioner. In the work of a genuine dramatic poet, the transitional passages in which the unnatural, or the contrived, enters in are the true measure of the poet's strength because they show whether he has the power to lift his whole conception above the accidental into the realm of the universal. For him the unnatural becomes an organic part of the total effect, while with lesser authors such matters are accepted as truth only reluctantly and with annoyance.

Therefore, in the production of a play everyone—the director, the scene designer, and the actor—must surmount the restrictions of naturalism. Actually, no one in real life behaves as our actors behave in the pieces which pretend to be true-to-nature imitations of reality. Moreover, a sort of conventionalization of natural behavior has been developing upon the stage. This is also discernable in the decoration of the scenes, even the most naturalistic. Between naturalism on the stage and style on the stage, there is less difference in kind than in degree. Since this is so, playhouses that possess artistic integrity are constantly impelled to work out these stylistic elements more strongly and completely. And even in the presentation of realistic drama they are likely to achieve a style which runs parallel to impressionism. By expressive emphasis on the vital point, by suggestively effective indication of the essential and only the essential, they will produce for the spectator the impression of the whole.

The theatre has always had a dual personality: one solemn and weighty, the other intimate and lively. Everyone occasionally desires to spend an evening at a comedy. And a person of cultivation should be assured that here too everything he hears and sees will be in harmony with the culture in which he lives. Beginnings toward this end are numerous. Their further development is made difficult by the fact that existing buildings and stages allow at most only a compromise with good taste. Such compromises are unrealistic. Whoever desires to put into practice the discoveries of the Artists' Theatre will have to create entirely new conditions, conditions which fulfill the basic functions of the theatre.

V

Drama

THE alterations which we find in the playhouse, in the auditorium, the stage, the scenery, and the manner of production are actually manifestations of a deeper and more fundamental transformation. These changes are the heralds of the new drama which calls upon us to prepare a place in which it can appear. The current literary drama is the cultural equivalent of the narrative paintings and genre pictures which were popular ten years ago. But just as today the cultivated European considers in painting nothing save pure artistic form, and just as he has freed himself in sculpture and in architecture from the consideration of all literary elements, so in estimating the drama he makes his evaluation solely on the basis of pure dramatic form.

The subject—of whatever sort it may be, whether grossly material or purely intellectual—is the most important factor in the literary drama of today. But for genuinely artistic drama the subject matter is only a means to an end. The drama should be enriched as much as possible by the themes and subject matter of real life. Yet these things are merely vehicles for dramatic form. Just as in painting, the subject, be it a pile of rubbish or the goddess Venus, is only the means to an end in the creation of artistic form. Genuine drama does not evade life but takes from it that which is significant. It concerns itself with basic principles of creation and makes them the starting point for forms in which these principles are brought to a more complete expression, to unity and to harmony with each other.

So drama brings about an enrichment of life, mindful of the purpose of all art which is to possess the soul and lift it above the accidental confines of the environment in which for the time being it is bound by the flesh, to make accessible to the spirit a new world, to enrich and rejoice mankind by making available a more complete experience —experience more intensive in joy and in sorrow, with deeper insight into the harmony of life. Any performance which brings us this understanding has genuine dramatic form.

The written drama is no more than a score from which the basic form of the work is ultimately apprehended by the thoughtful and discriminating intelligence of the audience. If this score in and of itself offers enjoyment to those who can read it, so much the better, but here, as in music, there will never be more than a few who can really follow the score. And so, for the great majority the drama only becomes the experience which they seek when the dramatist leaves his desk, when he remembers that he has nothing in common with literature, and only a few things with poetry, and that he himself must turn his hand to the stage. Just as the builder belongs at the site of his building, so the dramatist belongs in the theatre.

That movement which in plastic art has led to emancipation from the literary and the accidental has been called a secession. Now we shall also have a secession in dramatic art. This is the last field to be affected because such a movement presupposes a cultural refinement on a much wider scale than do, for instance, painting and sculpture. The attendance at the Artists' Theatre both in character and in numbers has proved that the German-speaking countries possess an extensive and discriminating public which recognizes that it is impossible to place the ruling theatrical literature of the day on a level with modern painting, that as a matter of fact the greatest antipathy exists between them.

For the literary theatre the dramatic art form is not the aim of the theatre but rather the means to an end; dramatic art is used specifically for the presentation of literary concepts, not of artistic ones.

It is easy to understand how such a theatre arose in the industrialized Germany of the eighties and nineties. The social struggles, the economic, ethical, and philosophical controversies which developed in the large industrial centers of the newly arisen Germany made use of the powerful publicity value of the theatre as a tribunal. Theories, slogans, causes were more effectively broadcast by the theatre than by press, parliament, or congress. Just as the church had once made use of the Passion plays to bring first hand information of the terrors of Hell and the Last Judgment to the full-blooded, exuberant people of the Middle Ages, so now the movements of the time, both radical and reactionary, availed themselves of the stage to force the spectators, through the most true-to-life representations possible, actually to experience all the mayhaps or mishaps which the author of the piece believed it necessary to describe or to discuss.

This particular characteristic of modern stage literature at the close of the last century should not be overlooked if one is to understand why it inevitably led to an energetic reaction on the part of the artistic element in the theatre. Obviously, literary excellence in a dramatic art form often exists. The great majority of important dramatic creations are, if one reads them in a book, also highly important literary works, but they need not be so necessarily. In Shakespeare's *As You Like It* the sum total of literary value is comparatively slight. Profound thoughts, unique solutions of ethical, metaphysical, or social problems, uncommon characters, psychological analyses—all those factors which are so highly esteemed in the popular literature of today are here scarcely to be found. It is an indefinable, peculiarly dramatic quality that makes this genuinely actable comedy sparkle with enduring brilliance, in spite of its conventional theme, a theme which Shakespeare found already established in tradition and did not even think it necessary to disguise.

Moreover, in the other works of Shakespeare the literary element is always used in the service of the dramatic form. As a matter of fact, it is sometimes used in such a way that, as Goethe was fond of insisting, even psychological truth and plausibility are consciously sacrificed for the benefit of the dramatic situation, that is, for the benefit of a higher, a more artistic truth.

Literary drama, on the other hand, does not desire to be theatrical. Its exponents and representatives despise the theatre and are horrified at specifically theatrical effects, conventions, forms, methods, and styles. The most scathing thing that a modern critic can say about a play is that it is theatrical. Still, one should not reproach our critics on that account. Whenever, in present-day drama, we encounter the theatrical, we find it used in so banal and so crude a fashion, in such a debased and ordinary way, and treated in such a dilettante fashion that one easily understands why serious critics condemn it.

A theatre which is not a theatre and does not wish to be one—is that not indeed a "*locus a non lucendo*," an innate absurdity? To be sure, no one was satisfied with such a theatre; neither the public which could only be brought to visit it by the unscrupulous invitations of suggestive advertising, nor the performers, nor the managers who were forced to put on hits of the lowest order, thus degrading the level of taste at which they would have liked to maintain their theatres. It was, therefore, inevitable that the literary drama should quickly become decadent, for in order to make up for the theatrical qualities which it lacked, the stage was obliged to adopt sensational features attractive to the masses. A scandal at the opening, the ban of the censor, a protest from the defenders of purity, an exposé of well-known personalities, such maneuvers as occur in connection with "forbidden novels," these were soon the only means by which a literary piece could attract attention. When these no longer worked, everything came to an end.

But no! There was still another way in which to help one's self—by the production. The literary piece suddenly began to deck itself out in historical costumes or mythical accoutrements; to invite in painters and decorators hoping that they would bring it favorable notice for effective stage pictures or for some new kind of aesthetic sensationalism. And so the literary piece would come hobbling out of the wings entirely supported by the production.

Because fashionable dramatic literature needs an elaborate production to cover its nakedness, it becomes the passionate enemy of. the Artists' Theatre and of every enterprise which is concerned with theatrical style. The dramatic form which a piece possesses in itself is, to be sure, much intensified by the new theatrical techniques. But, by the same token, the want of such inner form is more clearly distinguishable. It is therefore dangerous for the new stage to try to befriend literary pieces which have no inner dramatic form, for their formlessness and lifelessness are revealed as starkly as are the weaknesses and failings of the individual players.

Through Wilhelm Meister in the *Lehrjahre* Goethe says, "I wish the stage were as narrow as the rope of a tightrope dancer, so that clumsy people would not dare to venture on it." This applies to dramatists as well as to performers. One may properly consider a dramatist clumsy if he needs a lot of literary claptrap to make his piece effective.

From the smallest, simplest, most everyday human themes a real dramatic poet can develop a living organism, rhythmic and complete. He does not need the spice of paradox nor the exhortation of moralizing; he does not need philosophical reflections, psychological pyrotechnics, nor detailed and authentic representations of persons and places. All of these are elementary. They are merely building material. It does not matter whether the play is in verse or in prose, whether it deals with naturalism or idealism, world philosophy or tragedy. None of these things affects its quality, just as it is immaterial what a picture represents, what title it has, what stories are told about it. The quality rests in both cases solely on adherence to the laws of rhythm and design. In the drama this results in a psychical rhythmic movement with fixed caesura, pauses, beats, and measures. Only when this psychical rhythm is present do we become so absorbed in the events on the stage that these experiences become our own—the purpose for which we go to the theatre in the first place.

2

The real reason that theatrical drama has been attacked in a literary age is that its opponents could not achieve it. Just as in an age of literary painters, the Nazarines (Kaulbach, Hasenclever, and their contemporaries) inveighed against the ability to paint, because they themselves could not. In the days of the old masters there was no difference between literary and unliterary art. The painter understood and practiced his craft. The dramatist also was a thorough technician.

Shakespeare, the greatest dramatic poet of all time, knew no literary ambition and worked for a given stage, for specific players, for a particular audience, with due consideration for the business interests of his organization, and with a candid recognition of all these factors. He remained within the conventions of his calling, cared nothing for originality, depended as little as possible on literary devices in the handling of his dialogues, and preferred to take his plots from Plutarch or from the penny dreadfuls of his day. He took over the comic types which had been used for centuries upon the stage. He had nothing against Punch or a merry-andrew or any of the other clowns, buffoons, and jesters, each of whom is the veritable image of all that is unliterary. He showed his craftsman's pride, his ambition to excel as a technician, by precisely the way in which he used the most ordinary material of his trade, but used it in such uncommon ways as to win new charm for it. He rearranged it, abbreviated it, expanded and combined it. And all this in strict accordance with its structure.

Every successful clown, acrobat, tightrope walker, and juggler has in like fashion certain "tricks"—little, precise, delicate deviations from the common practice of his kind. By these he imprints on the familiar form new charm, new meaning, and new value. So Shakespeare, too, made use of the ordinary dramatic material of his day and was probably not conscious of giving new form to the subject matter that he shared with his fellow craftsmen. As a matter of fact, the boundary which separates him from the other commercial dramatists of his epoch is quite indefinite. There is much doubt as to whether certain pieces should be attributed to him or to others. And as for the "authentic" pieces, it has only been by scientific research on the part of a posterity no longer capable of careless enjoyment that the fire of "genius" burning in his heart has been laid bare. Through the ages, this conception of genius has not always coincided with our native cultural instincts.

The idea of genius was first formulated by the preromanticists of the eighteenth century, at the time when the pursuit of culture had become divergent, and it was thought necessary to differentiate between genuine artists and poets ("geniuses") and second-rate ones. The latter were really not artists at all but were merely men who used the resources and techniques of art to present certain theories of culture. They no longer had anything in common with the tradition of craftsmanship in the arts.

The dictatorship of literature over painting, architecture, and drama was unknown in earlier times. One made no distinction between original artists and others, for only the original, only the talented, became artists by profession. Dürer, Shakespeare, Rembrandt, Molière, Mozart were exactly the same as their fellow craftsmen, working contentedly for their daily needs, happy perhaps that they were able to please the fastidious better than their rivals. They may have been secretly a little proud that, in their more successful productions, they were able to add qualities beyond the requirements of the most exacting critics. To such men, a concerted clamor in the clouds of aesthetic metaphysics and a premature basking in the radiance of immortal glory such as is customary today was quite unknown. Furthermore, the very notion of immortality is originally a literary idea. Where there is no literature there is also no "immortal fame."

The creators of the noblest monuments of Egyptian and Moorish architecture, of Romanesque and Gothic cathedrals, and of many of the greatest masterpieces do without immortality, which shows how comparatively worthless it is and how little to be depended upon. The fact that a creative genius, by whose work the contemporary practice of art is raised to a higher plane, is inwardly conscious of his own superior strength in comparison with that of fellow craftsmen who are still clinging to the past, does not prevent him from being classified by himself and by others as a member of a very definite coterie of technical experts and rated as such. Hysterical evaluations, such as are the order of the day in our culturally confused and unstable time, were formerly quite unthinkable—evaluations whereby a Cornelius, a Richard Wagner, or a Böcklin is venerated as a direct manifestation of God Himself, and anyone is ridiculed who dares to place such artists in the same class with "common" craftsmen such as Schwind, Johann Strauss, or Leibl.

Formerly, every artist, even the most highly endowed, was judged by the aim, the technical perfection, and the general cultural value of his work. Neither Phidias nor Michelangelo, Titian nor Velásquez, Rubens nor Rembrandt, Aeschylus nor Sophocles, Shakespeare nor Goethe, Bach nor Gluck nor Mozart thought of withholding himself from the tasks and requirements prescribed by the cultural needs of his time. On the contrary, the masters and their pupils found, in this devotion to the task of supplying the needs of their times, precisely that beneficent compulsion which led them to the full development of their style.

For the old masters dramas, like pictures, were strictly technical problems. Dramatic tasks were performed, not in the delusion of bestowing upon the human race a highly personal manifestation of the Godhead, but merely with the idea of doing a useful piece of work. The style was developed in accordance with the purpose of the work, just as it is in architecture.

And so there was no fundamental difference between literary drama and mere dialogue, any more than there was a fundamental difference between painting which was specifically artistic and that which was not. Even the simple house painters who decorated the walls of the peasant houses in Bavaria and the Tirol with pictures of the saints were working in the field of art and were considered in the same category as the painter Holbein of Augsburg who afterwards became world renowned. Likewise, great dramatists who later became famous wrote simple little plays such as were desired by their patrons for their own amusement or for entertainment on the celebration of special occasions.

The same dramatist who created *Hamlet* also furnished farces in the customary pattern, modest pieces in which there is nothing except what the actors need to entertain their public. The same dramatist who left us *Faust* wrote, for the court society of Weimar, dialogues which were performed in their private theatre and on their garden stage in the castle park. Such works as *Tasso* and *Iphigenie* grew out of such pieces, and the author took great pains to develop these stage entertainments according to the existing theatrical conventions. *Bürgergeneral*, *Grosskophta*, *Geschwister*, and *Stella* are examples. Nor did he consider himself too important an artist to write opera texts if his Weimar theatre needed them. In short, Goethe saw the playwright quite modestly and in his true proportions. If the author of theatre pieces performed his tasks in accordance with artistic principles he was praised; if he did not, he was censured. It did not matter whether or not he was able to embellish his work with such refinements as philosophy, poetry, wit, or intellectual discussion. In considering all these fortuitous elements, what counted was whether or not they were controlled by the technical tools of art. Their functional significance in the dramatic structure of the piece was the only justification for their existence.

Shakespeare, for instance, does not hesitate, since the dramatic form demands it, to make his Hamlet a good Christian believing in Heaven, Hell, Purgatory, and the Last Judgment, and at the same time to show him as a materialistic atheist. And so, in genuine drama, even so basic a thing as the psychological nature of the characters is developed according to purely artistic truth. The characters, like every other element in a play, should be subject to the laws of art and held to be true only in so far as they obey such laws. We often meet a parallel instance in plastic art when the sculptor, the fresco painter, or the caricaturist foreshortens the human figure or represents it in proportions which contradict the scientifically exact specifications of reality, but which artistically are nevertheless undeniably true because they are in harmony with the particular proportions which are right for that specific work of art. Everyone knows that the effectiveness of a work of art depends on this organic transformation of the appearance of reality into artistic form. It can, however, only be accomplished by one who is thoroughly familiar with realistic forms, with the characteristics of the material, and with the technique of the particular art. Only that painter paints artistically who knows exactly the value of the colors, their relation to each other, how to handle the foreground and background, warm and cold tints, lights and shadows, curves and planes as materials for the building of his picture. The literary painter of the seventies and eighties had not the slightest notion of all this. He did not care about the form of his picture, but instead used the tools of painting for the communication of philosophy, the teaching of history, the telling of anecdotes, the illumination of moral or psychological problems, the debate of controversial questions, the disclosure of human weaknesses and social foibles—in short, for exactly the same purpose for which the literary dramatists of today make use of the stage equipment and the living actor. Literary dramatists do not need, therefore, to be familiar with the true nature of theatrical art any more than the literary painters needed to know the fundamental principles of artistic creation.

What the literati understand by "knowledge of the stage" is knowledge not of the resources and nature of theatrical art but of the tricks and practices that must be employed to drain the theatrical elements from literature and make them usable in the theatre. For this reason most men of letters are incapable of judging actors and their accomplishments. A great many clever critics in the analysis of a novel or a picture show both intellectual acumen and discriminating taste but when judging an actor are completely at a loss and blunder in the most astounding fashion. This happens because they are not accustomed to think of the actor and the theatre as parts of an independent art but only as the instruments of literature. Hence the everlasting talk of "interpretation," "analysis," "psychological investigation," and "intellectual artists"; and hence the storm of protest if an actor dares to "act," or a comedian to "play comedy," or a theatre to be "theatrical."

According to the literary point of view which is so common among "educated" people, art and artists are not intended to fulfill their independent functions but only to advertise literature as effectively as possible. An actor who today would react with temperament and unreserved abandon to the creative urge within him would be treated like a criminal. He would be "outré," a "shameless ranter," "old fashioned." The result is that actors of undoubtedly original talent emasculate themselves, crush all creative strength and independent force within them so that they may be more accommodating interpreters of the esoteric offerings of the literati.

The tyranny of the director in the modern drama is also explained by the surrender of the theatre to literature. The actor needs a ringmaster if he is not to give in to the theatrical impulse, the creative urge, within himself; if he is to fulfill the function that has been forced upon him as a walking illustration of a literary text. The more talented he is, the more of an actor, the more he needs someone to crack the whip and to keep him in line. Therefore, in the era of the literary stage, the director is the dictator, the dominating personality, the admired virtuoso, the highest in command, who has the actor under his thumb and before whom even the literati crawl in the dust—for without this great magician the theatre would be lost.

3

The theatre of the old masters, the theatre of traditional culture, never knew the director in the sense in which we know him. Direction was formerly a technical function more in line with the work of our present-day stage managers. The artistic and intellectual decisions which today are loaded on the director lay, in so far as the theatre exercised them at all, in the hands of the author. Formerly, the playwright was a craftsman, a competent man of the theatre, though also at times, in the best sense an amateur. But never, in any sense, a dilettante. Many poets bore this relation to the theatre, among them Goethe. But the poet was always a dramatist. And so the hard and fast line between original drama and the reworking and adaptation of older pieces did not exist. New plays were often nothing more than simple rearrangements of older dramas, reworking of material long familiar in the tradition of the repertory. This is true of Goethe's *Faust* and of most of Shakespeare's plays. Both Goethe and Schiller translated and adapted older pieces for the Weimar theatre and both embodied in themselves the ancient unity of poet-dramatist-director.

When there was no such person as a director it was customary to work out many problems solely on the basis of tradition. The division of roles into "parts" (First Lead, Character Actor, Heavy, Comic, and the like) is a relic of the old stage tradition by which many tasks were made easier by the functioning of automatic rules, tasks which today are undertaken by the director. One of them, for example, was what we understand as interpretation. This was not then left to the individuality of the director but was a matter of tradition, an unwritten law of style embodied in the members of the troupe from childhood on and renewed and refreshed from time to time by the influence of such poet-dramatists. This influence gradually radiated far from the scene of the dramatist's endeavors, mostly through those performing his works. The most historic examples of this are to be found in the spread of "classicism" through Goethe and Schiller and the "Bayreuth style" of Wagner.

Even today every really talented actor possesses in

himself certain strongly traditional qualities, though they are mostly unconscious and involuntary. Talent, particularly genuine "theatrical blood," searches instinctively for the soil of tradition from which arises a wealth of formal material that saves him a great deal of useless trouble with the first stages of preparation and enables him to concentrate his strength on the creative development of his roles. Strong talent can follow this technique because it need never have any fear of falling into a stereotyped pattern, whereas the dilettante, conscious of his weakness, avoids traditions because he cannot master them; he is subdued by them and stamped as affected and imitative. In the theatre, as in every art, tradition is the foundation; freedom in artistic creation is not attained by avoiding it but by grasping it boldly and commanding it.

4

There is, to be sure, a certain false tradition, an old routine, which is handed down like a hereditary disease. To this tradition belongs the conventional pattern of Gretchen according to the style of china chimney-piece ornaments. Goethe despised such sentimentalism. Yet the Renaissance Gretchen in all her blue-eyed blondness and sugary sweetness bobbed and curtsied on the German stage for generations. This sentimental symbol was finally shattered by Fritz Erler in the Artists' Theatre. Here, Lina Lossen was allowed to recreate Goethe's Gretchen with simplicity, sensitivity, and artistic integrity.

Actually, literary writers had little quarrel with the sentimentalism and the tastelessness of such theatre practice and did not really mind when the old masters gradually declined and public interest in the pedantry and dusty decay of the routine productions waned. The old masters were as dangerous as rivals as they had been as examples. So everyone happily agreed that the "vapid sentimentality" of Schiller had become "impossible," and it was conceded in the cafés that Goethe was an "undramatic author." How unfortunate that such satisfactory decisions should be upset by the establishment of the Artists' Theatre in Munich where the performances of *Faust* released torrents of unprecedented praise!

The Artists' Theatre fought and conquered false tradition, but the literati contended against genuine tradition and were overthrown. Even when the representatives of the literary movement again took up the old masters, they did so only to rob them of their real dramatic and theatrical nature, to impoverish them and turn them into "literature." They pretended to be against the mechanical distribution of parts according to type and demanded that Karl Moor be played, not as a juvenile according to the tradition which goes back to Schiller himself, but as a neurasthenic anarchist; that Franz Moor be acted not as a theatrical villain, but as a perverted sadist; Amalia not as a sensitive dreamer but as a neurotic; Joan of Arc not as mystical and heroic but as hysterical and psychopathic. In this way, tradition is indeed destroyed, but at the same time the art of the theatre, the characters and the play, are destroyed also, for characters can never be convincing if they are to represent something quite different from what the poet intended.

Moreover, a performance so at variance with the usage and tradition of the theatre is practically impossible to achieve. This is true not only with regard to the older pieces, but with regard to the modern literary drama as well. It is proved by the fact that only one single isolated performance is successful according to the precepts of the literati. It is something which anyone may discover for himself by attending two performances of the same production.

At the première, all habitual first-nighters are agreed that the great director, "demiurgos," has succeeded with his usual touch of genius (the works of the poet are created for the great directors, not the other way around!) in completely melting up his acting material and, in his creative hands, kneading it like a lump of clay into an expression of his own superdirector's, highly personal, hyperdifferentiated, neoindividuality! There is no doubt about it. At the première, at the first and second repetitions, critics can notice nothing about the actors to suggest that they have been cast for their parts according to type, nothing of unconscious stylization according to tradition. At these performances the world appears newborn and "glorious as on the first day." Habitués and representatives of the press rise to heights of rapture and only the high-priest director smiles, perhaps a little maliciously, for he knows, if anyone does, what is behind it all. Ah yes, to gratify the fashionable literati he has once more murdered the drama—but he knows very well that it will rise again upon the third day.

Fortunately no qualified critic or literary snob ever comes to a third performance—or to any subsequent one. He would be disgraced to be caught at any performance save the première, when he can be with his own kind. But let us slip into a thirteenth performance or a hundredth one. Let us hide in the darkness of a box and observe the original cast. We scarcely recognize it. All the director's transcendental and personal contributions have disappeared. Here they all are together again: the trusty old "character actor," the "hero," the "ingénue," the "rube," the "young lover." All the traditional types are portrayed with an individuality which is, perhaps, notably original but which is still as recognizable as ever. The drama, the material, has had its revenge! And then they say the performance has "slumped." In my opinion, the slump occurred when the theatrical material was misused in the first place, when it was used for a purpose which was untheatrical, when the characteristics of the material, the dignity of tradition, and the life force of the actor were all denied, when the public was tricked and given not the bread of art but the stone of literature. An architect or a sculptor who would deny his material would never be taken seriously again. In the theatre the reverse is true.

A festival house such as the Artists' Theatre is obliged to give each of its performances as though it were a première. Our audiences come from all lands where the German tongue is spoken and from many foreign countries, as each one's desire for a Munich season leads him to the Isar. For this reason, discriminating critics are to be found at all performances. At each one, even at the last, an influential critic and a group of important artists may be present. It is not possible for the manager of a festival house to collect the people who pass judgment on his calling into one group and on one particular evening to put before them a menu which is never again to be equaled in quality, savor, and service. The forms which the festival performance chooses for its productions must hold for all presentations except, of course, for unavoidable variations in things that are unimportant or accidental. And so a festival performance must have a genuinely theatrical art form which is deeply rooted in the flesh and blood of the performers.

5

The dramatist has in principle the same relation to the actor as a sculptor to the block of stone out of which he is to carve a statue. With heightened imagination he attends, he observes, he contemplates the latent possibilities of form inherent in the material and finally brings them forth. And just as one senses in Michelangelo's *Night* the block of marble from which—its weight and substance skillfully preserved—the statue has been chiseled, so in every role one must be able to feel the personality of the performer if the figure is to appear artistically alive. If one does away with this personality, if one loses this relationship to life in order to impose an arbitrarily thought-out literary construction or pattern, the result is an automaton which, after a time, ceases to function.

The dramatist must have, either as a birthright or as a result of careful cultivation, a delicate understanding of the possibilities of form which are inherent in the personalities of the performers and must be able to create his performances out of them, just as a sculptor must have an exact knowledge of different sorts of stone or a painter must be able to paint "from his palette." The purely literary dramatists, on the other hand, are similar to the members of the now passé school of sculptors and architects who in the isolation of their studios without any knowledge of or consideration for their materials sketched their ideas on scratch paper and then handed them over to helpers to be carried out by them as best they could. Just as the figures which they conceived without any vital relationship to the material, the atmosphere, and the surroundings appear lifeless, and just as the buildings they planned according to some arbitrary literary style now stand there stark, stupid, and expressionless, so literary drama, which is not created out of theatrical material, is always untheatrical and therefore not effective in an artistic sense even though it be performed according to the most penetrating and precise psychological laws.

The dramatist cannot, to be sure, know every individual player personally, any more than the sculptor can know every individual block of stone. And it is not necessary that he should, for the nature of artistic expression is simplification, the return from the accidental to the universal. The artist needs only a knowledge of the types of his materials. The sculptor who models a statue for execution in linden wood need not know every individual piece of linden, but he must know with certainty the typical qualities of all linden wood, how it reacts to the knife, how it is grained, what contingencies to expect in its structure, how it darkens with age. So the creative dramatist needs a knowledge of types, of the ever-recurrent characteristics in the human material which is at his command as a means of expression. As Hoffmann has said, "The playwright must know not only man but mankind."

A primitive system of differentiating the actors, which is based on age-long experience, is found in the customary division into types of parts, something not to be exterminated. This, to be sure, is not in itself sufficient for the dramatist; it serves more as an aid to the manager of a commercial theatre, to the producer, and to the trade. It nevertheless has its foundations deep in the nature of theatrical art and is a part of the knowledge of the material which anyone needs who wants to give life to a theatrical form of art. It defines the possibilities and shows how they may be developed most advantageously. It is a theatrical device for the handling of theatrical material, and this material as a whole is what we understand by the word theatre.

But first we must have a theatre in which we can live and create and which represents the general level of our culture. Therefore, all the creative forces which support our culture must co-operate in the theatre. Formerly, if one wanted to be theatrical one was obliged to sink to the comparatively low level of culture on which the average theatre existed. In the Artists' Theatre it is possible to be both theatrical and in good taste.

6

But let us be quite fair to the literary drama. It grew in the beginning out of the maladjustment between the level of theatrical culture and the demands of taste which the elite, the highly educated, made upon the drama. When the drama sank to the level of theatricalism it became practically useless to people of good taste. "Let us free ourselves from this theatricalism which even Lessing, Schiller, Goethe, and Immermann were not always able to ennoble," it was said. Therefore the following generations, first Kleist, then Grillparzer, Hebbel, and Ibsen, tore themselves free from the current theatrical practices.

They created without consideration for the material which seemed only to drag them down. They became "purely literary," leaving the theatre to work its way up to their level. Moreover, it was the foremost theatrical men of the previous period who made it possible by the end of the nineteenth century to offer these poets homes for their dramas in some of the theatres of their day.

But the theatrical producers were only able to do this by following the leading poets in freeing the theatre more and more from theatricalism and by placing the material—that is, the theatre and the actors—in the service of the literary drama. In this way, the literary drama arose, and in this way it has become fully justified in the estimation of the intellectual world. This we should not deny even though we ourselves are occupied in solving another problem of which the literary stage did not even recognize the existence; that is, the problem of endowing the theatre with all the creative force of modern cultural endeavor and of bringing it (following its own structural principles and emphasizing honestly its purpose and its material) to the same cultural level as that which is occupied by painting, engineering, landscape architecture, and other applied arts.

As we now understand it, a part of this theatre is the dramatic literature. It belongs to the theatre as does the actor. It grows out of the theatre, out of the material, just as the statue grows out of the block of marble without losing its basic origins in the material. It rises to the highest and freest intellectual eminence whence it directs the theatre toward new and progressive development. And these principles of development are then not of literary but of theatrical heritage, growing out of the material and for the material, out of the theatre for the theatre.

But the dramatic poet who looks at the situation from this point of view soon encounters difficulties. The author, alert to literary values, especially if he possesses a certain journalistic talent for the effective elucidation of actual problems, or a certain vaudeville talent for sensationalism and hokum, finds the doors of the best playhouses thrown wide open to him. On the other hand, the purely dramatic poet, although he is much more theatrical than the literary dramatist, must first lay hands on the theatre and reorganize it to suit his especial needs. In this connection the education of the performer in the artistic presentation of poetry is particularly important. Goethe wrote in his journal of February 1800, "In the Weimar theatre we labored ceaselessly to bring back to favor that rhythmical declamation which has been so much neglected in the past; which has, indeed, been almost completely lost to the German stage."

There may be some one who will reproach us by saying: If Goethe, Schiller, and all the other great ones of a hundred years ago were not successful, you will certainly never reach the goal. Let them examine the records and discover how it happened that the plans of Goethe, Schiller, and Schinkel—which were identical with ours—came to be shattered. There were several reasons. First, Germany was poor, and money was scarce even at the German courts. Secondly, the primitive means of communication did not permit the friends of art to gather, every year from everywhere, in one city and in one theatre for a season, as is now the case in Bayreuth and in Munich. And finally, the development of the plastic arts had been almost abandoned. In order to create in design and decoration the values which are essential for our sort of stage and which were most earnestly sought by Goethe as well as by Schinkel and Immermann, one needs a very advanced and creative culture.

At that time, things looked particularly bleak in that direction. All the arts, architecture included, had become literary. The plastic artists had rejected life and so stood helpless before the tasks which Goethe and Schiller set them. A single exception was the great genius Friedrich Schinkel, whose industry in building left him only occasional time now and then to dedicate to the theatre. But today we have a plastic art which is more than adequate —an art which demonstrated in the Munich Artists' Theatre with complete success that it is equal to the most extensive problems of the stage. And so the dramatist is no longer required to use the theatre as a mere makeshift device for the promulgation of literature. He is free to be theatrical—if he can be.

The time has come when we must face the responsibility of fulfilling our purpose. What is our purpose? Perhaps no one has expressed it more forcefully than E. Th. A. Hoffmann, that wise person who has said the last word on so many subjects: "There is no higher purpose in art than to kindle in man that kind of joy which frees him from all earthly torment, from all the oppressive weight of everyday life, and so exalts him that, lifting his head with pride and joy, he looks at God, yes, even communes with Him. In my opinion, the inspiration of this joy is the sole purpose of the theatre. It is this capacity for the comprehension of the world as an entity, this ability to regard the happenings of human existence not as unrelated incidents but as parts of a perfect order—each deeply woven into the fabric of the whole—this gift for grasping the inner significances of such phenomena and reproducing them in living colors, this is what constitutes the genius of the true dramatic poet."

VI

Opera

LET us repudiate the literary poses with which we have been so abominably bored for decades. Let us honestly admit that we want the theatre to be once more entirely theatrical and the opera once more operatic. In the opera dramatic effect is created by a body of sound and particularly by that of the singing voice. Therefore in opera conditions obtain which are so different from those that exist in the spoken drama or the pantomime, and indeed the ends to be served are so divergent, that one can almost say: The more suitable a building is for opera, the more unsuitable it is for a play.

If here and there both opera and drama must be produced in the same house, that is a matter of necessity from which both suffer. But if playhouses continue to be built after the pattern of opera houses, that is arrant stupidity. The theatre requires a shallow stage; the opera needs a deep one because there must be room for the chorus; and the size of the opera chorus depends on the musical task it has to perform. In opera the chorus not only must suggest the optical impression of a crowd as in a play and the illusion of a crowd as created by sound, but it must also take account of the relative strength of the individual voices. One cannot confine the problem to the impression made upon the eyes alone.

Opera which is intended to be real opera—not music drama in the sense of Wagner's combination works of art—is at home on the wing stage and should stay there, for the wing is the only architectural unit by which a deep scene may be knit together and at the same time masked at the sides. But one should definitely abandon the idea of imitating with wings a bit of nature, an effort which in any circumstance is unconvincing. There should be a return to the original treatment of the wing set. This treatment was thoroughly organic and architectural. One should honestly admit that the wing is nothing but a strip of material and should use this strip to unite the depth in exactly the same way that wings of masonry and columns are employed in interior architecture or that wings are used in landscape gardening in the form of hedges bordering on a canal, a road, or a lawn so that they mask the view at the sides and guide the eye toward the depth while leaving the passage open.

When these architectural methods of dealing with space are to be decoratively distinguished from one another so as to indicate definite localities (landscapes, interiors, streets, caverns, woods), we are faced with a problem which has never been solved—and which never will be solved without the help of those who alone are equal to it, the painter and designer. For them such a problem is not difficult; it is quite a matter of course.

For them the depth of the wings together with the joining soffits represents nothing more than a repetition of the inner proscenium of the Artists' Theatre.

For this inner proscenium as well as for the wings, the strictest neutrality is necessary so that the performer, no matter where he may be on the stage, may not only appear as the principal feature in the scene but also that he may always make the right impression. If one treats the last wings as though they represented a landscape miles away, the performer between them will look like a monster, since he does not become correspondingly smaller. Therefore, a simple treatment which is both ornamental and symbolic is the only one possible on the wing stage, a frescoed style after the manner of the Pompeian wall decorations or the ceiling paintings of the baroque period. These individual features are then given meaning by the background and are thus united in a single harmonious design. At the same time they bring to the scene in question an illusion of the necessary landscape or the architectural conception. This illusion, however, is not the inorganic one of the panorama but a consistent, artistic illusion such as was born of the opera itself from the very beginning. The proof of this contention may be established by an examination of the Teatro Farnese at Piacenza.

Nevertheless, only opera in the true sense—opera which is really opera and attempts to be nothing else—will achieve its most satisfactory effects on this sort of stage. Music dramas such as Wagner's cannot be transplanted onto such a stage. One need only run through the score of such a performance, strongly in contrast as it is to the operatic style, to notice that changes in scenery are expected to parallel those of the musical tone-pictures painted by the orchestra.

Wagner's *Ring* is in large measure robbed of its effect if the water of the Rhine does not flow, if the atmospheric illusion upon the stage does not correspond exactly to the mood of the music. Music drama maintains much the same relationship to the scene as does the literary drama, because it also is a mixture in which, along with artistic elements, are mingled many literary qualities which do not lend themselves to physical interpretation unless certain detailed, visual aids gave the eyes instruction and explanation. It is, however, superfluous to worry about the music drama, since Wagner wrote an exact description of the way he wanted it produced, and people are only too eager to follow his directions.

2

The task of the future will be to design a type of scenery suitable to the unliterary music drama, the severely stylized opera as it was developed by Gluck, Mozart, Beethoven, Auber, Bizet, Verdi, Offenbach, and lately by a new school of younger German composers such as Anton Beer-Walbrunn. The effort which the Artists' Theatre expended in this area was successful beyond all expectations. The public even evinced a tender regard for Gluck's *May Queen;* for this, Mottl deserves great credit because he dared to present that charming little shepherd's play as chamber-music opera. This was possible because of the acoustics of the Artists' Theatre. As a result, the public (which had been almost deafened by the volume of sound at the Wagnerian performances in the Prince Regent's Theatre) was all the more enchanted by the graceful lightness of the *May Queen.* The performance made use only of the space within the inner proscenium of the Artists' Theatre.

If one imagines this space many times repeated in depth, one has an understanding of the opera stage as here proposed. And in this connection we should not forget that Friedrich Schinkel, a hundred years ago, suggested the same scenic form and, pencil in hand, actually designed such a stage for such operas as *The Magic Flute*, *Undine*, and *Armide.* Moreover, he located the action of the play within a neutral proscenium which was cut off at the back by a single scenic painting. From this shallow stage he also developed a deeper opera stage by repeating as often as necessary the pairs of columns at the sides joined by a bridge at the top so as to prevent the eyes from penetrating at the top and sides into the workrooms. Thus he concentrated attention on the single decorative background. He himself says,

The deep proscenium will be most useful because of its flat broad ceiling, and because of the inclosure at the sides, since most of the speaking will take place between its walls. On the stage itself one sees at both sides, instead of wings and borders, permanent wall draperies which prevent the members of the audience who occupy the side seats from seeing behind the scenes. The walls thus appear to the audience as continuations of the curtains. Above them they also carry special lighting apparatus.

The practice of contracting the stage opening by lowering the ceiling of the inner proscenium and perhaps of the following pair of wings will only be possible in opera in a rather limited way so long as opera houses do not also have auditoriums in the amphitheatre form. In the balconied theatre too many people would be deprived of their view of the principal acting space. But we must always remember that the opera is really opera and has its own conventions, which are by no means identical with those of Wagnerian music drama—as Wagner himself realized and continually emphasized. Just because the music drama, like the play, may need the amphitheatre, it does not follow that the opera cannot be better taken care of in an auditorium with balconies. The opera created the theatre-with-boxes as the functional form best suited to itself. It must therefore accept the disadvantages inherent in this form, for the dramatic effect of opera is chiefly manifest in sound, and this effect is often so overwhelming that many operagoers often intentionally turn their glances away from the stage.

The dramatic music of the great masters takes possession of us to such an extent that it can even suggest ideas of decoration. It is immaterial, for instance, whether or not at a performance of *Figaro* the stage opening is made smaller, for the music itself will evoke in us the thought of a rococo boudoir. Similarly the moving, fateful tones that accompany the appearance of the commander in *Don Juan* inevitably widen the scene to suit our mood even though the stage be on the smallest scale. Scenic art will never be able adequately to construct for us the columned halls that rise in our imagination when in *The Magic Flute* Sarastro sings his "In these holy halls" or the chorus of priests begins to chant, "Oh, Isis and Osiris." All that plastic art can do here is to exercise the utmost restraint in the creation of the stage pictures so that the images that arise in every listener, filling him with emotion, may not be dimmed or restricted.

Another experience which is familiar to everyone who possesses the musical temperament necessary for the enjoyment of opera is that of the physical transformation of the singers under the influence which the music exerts on the emotional state of the audience. A singer is always as beautiful as her singing. It is only in the first moment that bodily shortcomings register. As the musical drama progresses, the performer looks to the inward eye of the beholder more and more like the figure called forth by the musical concept—always supposing, of course, that creative music and worthwhile vocal performances are forthcoming without any annoying affectations.

The worse the music and the worse the singing, the more we are tempted to look at the performer from the point of view of the drama—and as we do so all artistic values vanish, and opera becomes an absurdity.[1] Hence the meticulous care which in opera is given to insure a clear, clean-cut use of the musical and vocal means of expression. This careful concern is in sharp contrast to the drama, for the average theatre has to get along with only a poor approximation of it. Because in opera the scenic effects are so influenced by the musical expression, we do not feel it necessary to follow closely the events upon the stage. At times we even desire to be free of them, to lean back with closed eyes and submit ourselves entirely to the keen delight which the music has magically aroused in us. In a box we are the least disturbed at this—consequently the theatre with boxes will never disappear as long as there is opera.

An opera captures the mind and spirit of the audience in a way quite different from that of a play, and therefore the architecture of the opera house must have a different form from that of the playhouse. Moreover, enthusiasm for the opera cannot be heightened by a reformation undertaken blindly and heedlessly, according to sundry aesthetic maxims. Here too the need is to be objective and to make only such changes as are suited to the material. All that is required is to clear away the distracting rubbish with which the false ideals of a parvenu age have covered up a tradition that is at bottom dignified and sound.

In this, not only the managers and builders of the opera houses, the stage directors, and technical directors must co-operate but also, and most especially, the conductors of the orchestras. Many distinguished conductors, because of a misunderstanding of Wagner, would like to interpret every opera as a music drama. Because they admire Wagner so much, they make the mistake of thinking that every drama that uses music as a means of expression is a sort of inferior forerunner of the music drama. They assume that Gluck, Mozart, Beethoven, and Weber really wanted to write not operas but music dramas, that, unfortunately, they or their librettists lacked the poetical talent which distinguished Wagner and that, otherwise, they would have abandoned the idea of opera. How wrong this opinion is needs no proof. Mozart and Beethoven worked intensively on the structure of their productions and wanted them to be exactly what they are; namely, opera.

3

And so there is nothing to quarrel about: the music drama is a new and secondary species of dramatic creation brought about by the union of opera and literature. It has particular requirements. It is madness to suppose that one of these species will ever absorb the other.

We should therefore reacquaint ourselves with the culture and requirements of real opera. These are still quite ascertainable. There was, however, a period when throughout the world Wagner's success was comparable to that of P. T. Barnum and when it seemed to threaten the speedy extinction of the good old simple opera. But just as little as the gaudy Renaissance building style of 1880 could ultimately hinder the resumption of the good old traditional art of building, honest in its aims and its materials, just as little as the historical and symbolical literary painting of Kaulbach and Piloty held back the revival of the purely artistic principles of form developed by such masters as Feuerbach, Menzel, Marées, and Leibl, just so surely will the genuine opera, purely musical in style, come into its own alongside the literary music drama. It is deeply embedded in the cultural development of the ages.

The opera house of the future will offer as suitable a home for the opera as the Artists' Theatre does for the spoken drama. It will have a proper wing stage the depth of which will be extended by repetitions of the inner proscenium. It will have architectural wings joined together by ceiling pieces which carry the sources of light, and it will have a single unifying scenic wall at the back. Toward the front, a deep foreproscenium with a mobile orchestra will rise, and—perhaps not directly adjoining but following a plain wall space extending the whole height of the auditorium—a wide curved row of boxes with good acoustics and every comfort will be attached to a shallow raised amphitheatre. Satisfactory acoustics can only be achieved by lining the whole auditorium with wood.

Without making any concession to annoying virtuoso-like affectations, the opera of the future will permit in its style of production everything that is in any way helpful to the total effect. It will sweep from the stage the childish naturalism which nowhere appears more foolish than where people do not even talk, where speech itself is stylized in song. It will then become apparent that many characteristics which we have been condemning as abominable mannerisms in singers and prima donnas of volcanic temperament are, fundamentally, manifestations of thoroughly sound dramatic instincts, which only need to be properly directed to afford us the same full measure of satisfaction as was enjoyed by the distinguished audiences of Gluck, Mozart, Rossini, Auber, and Offenbach.

VII

Vaudeville

THE drama in its simplest form is rhythmic movement of the body in space. The variety, or vaudeville, stage is the place where drama in its simpler outlines is cultivated today in the form of dancing, acrobatics, juggling, sleight-of-hand, boxing and wrestling, exhibition of trained animals, musical dialogues (chanson), and what not. The dramatic effectiveness of such performances is indisputable, and the possibility of their artistic perfection is beyond question. We need only think of such dancers as Ruth St. Denis, of Saharet and Barison, of certain "eccentrics," various equestrian performers, and of Japanese acrobats to be convinced that when they have had training in the field of aesthetics these performers have every right to be called artists.

With them as with other theatrical performers, this is seldom the case. Therefore we find here, as everywhere else in this literary age, a snobbish withdrawal of the more highly cultivated and aesthetically developed. The vaudeville stage has been left to itself and to those who gained their livelihood by it. These are almost all children of the lower social orders who in the exercise of their natural-born or cultivated skills exhibit such aesthetic qualities as are considered most elegant in the circles in which they move. Everyone is acquainted with this magnificence, this excessively splendid taste, taste so grotesquely tasteless that it becomes almost charming. There is, indeed, something touching in this innocent delight in the most outrageous sham, in baubles, tinsel, bright colors, and frippery; in the childish unawareness that all this glitter, all this splendor, is in reality the deepest aesthetic destitution. What nevertheless strikes one most forcibly is the unfailing, vital impulse which maintains these artists in an enchanted world of make-believe, of joyous vitality, of dreamlike fantasy, and of a drama which has its roots in the body, in the animal instincts, and in the senses. It is these unintellectual theatre folk who really know most about the living functions of the drama. They thoroughly understand the joy which it should arouse in man, "so that he lifts his head high and proudly."

And so it is that among such performers more generally than in the rest of the theatre there may be found a striving for sure, clean work, for effective performances, and sound technique. Goethe meant what he said when he offered the tightrope dancer as a model for the actor, when he wished the stage were as narrow as a rope so that no awkward person could perform upon it. It was not without intent that in his *Lehrjahre* Goethe contrasted the artist Mignon, with her captivating egg dance, to the untrained, disorganized, dilettante actors who fumbled about uncertainly in their efforts to play *Hamlet* without having mastered their craft as the childlike Mignon had mastered the technique of her dance.

One easily understands why cultivated Germans, especially artists, have always favored the vaudeville stage and have sometimes preferred it to the theatre. But because of this preference they have complained the more emphatically of its shortcomings in matters of taste. They determined to reform it. And they set about making it as literary as the theatre itself. There was indeed a literary flavor to the very slogan with which they entered the field. They called their reform the Super Stage. And Nietzsche, the idol of the literati, was arbitrarily made its sponsor. They began to agitate for turning the variety stage into a stall for the sale of literature. Countless unread rhymsters hoped for golden days from this trend and cultivated a "grotesque note" so as to snatch from the Super Stage a percentage of that popularity of which they had previously been so contemptuous. They formed an alliance with those conscientious idealists who wanted to educate people in art, and they reformed away with great zeal.

Even the dance was reformed, and the public was lectured about it. They were told how much "purer" was the joy to which certain priestesses of the dance were anxious to educate them than was the grossly erotic charm of the common diva of the boards. The literary, learned, almost archaeological Miss Duncan was the star of this movement. The "Simplicissimus-style" was borrowed from the pages of Munich's funny paper and introduced into the cabarets. In short, reform became so literary that there were soon more literati than audience.

Meanwhile the real variety shows, which thousands upon thousands were attending nightly, went on as before. The public at large, and with them the vaudeville artists, betrayed not the least inclination to allow themselves to be educated by the Super Stage. They wanted only to be amused, and they found nothing less amusing than literature.

2

In spite of this, another influence succeeded, at least in certain instances, in affecting the vaudeville stage. This influence was inherent in the general artistic culture of Munich. It first made organized overtures toward vaudeville through the *Elf Schafrichter* (Eleven Executioners). Here were ballads sung by Frank Wedekind, chansons by Robert Kothe, certain grotesque numbers by Delvard, and scenes from Gumppenberg's *Tragödie in einem Satze* (Tragedy in One Sentence) which were executed with dramatic pantomime and acrobatics. This was real vaudeville, real in material and in technique, conceived in a thoroughly artistic fashion and shorn of cliché.

The close connection with the so-called "higher" art manifested itself in the person of several of these Executioners: Ernst Stern appeared as a sketch artist (*Schnellmaler*), Kothe brought back singing to the lute, a noble form of entertainment, which has too long been shoved aside by the epidemic of concert warblers and piano pests. Under the leadership of Falckenberg and Greiner, the simple impressionism which later received recognition in the Artists' Theatre was used here in the costuming as well as in the scenery. These are examples which show that the vaudeville stage does not need to be considered a lesser art by comparison with the higher art of the theatre, any more than does applied art in comparison with painting and sculpture.

Another form of variety entertainment which in Munich has risen to a high level is the "Toy" theatre. Such was the Puppet Theatre of Paul Brann, where artists like Taschner, Salzmann, Wackerle, and Bradl offered something close to perfection. Here the decor was of a high order, particularly when the scene design was kept simple and the playing space uncluttered so that the puppets could stand out strongly, and whenever the puppets themselves were designed without too much detail. The Puppet Theatre, incidentally, has also made occasional excursions into literature. But it has always kept its own style, getting its effects by delicate manipulation and exemplifying that earnest aspiration of the vaudeville artist to perfect technique for its own sake. The art of the puppeteer has been developed here according to the ancient traditions of Munich, and it has risen to a height which deserves great respect—perhaps no less respect than the technique of an eminent pianist.

At any rate, it may be seen from the beginnings already noted that, inspired by the creative spirit which is so strong in the artistic life of Munich, the variety stage will soon be up to the mark. Perhaps progress will be more rapid here than in the "big theatre," because Munich's artistic circles are full of variety talent, as one may soon perceive at any studio entertainment or artists' party. There is hardly a vaudeville number of which there are not amateur virtuosos among the Munich artists.

But if we set out to perfect a scheme by which vaudeville and art may be unified, we must make sure that vaudeville not only does not resign any of its functional and technical value, but that by embracing certain tenets of art it may be strengthened in the expression of its own characteristics and its own essential qualities. So, in principle, that thing must happen which, through the Munich Artists' Theatre, has already happened for the theatre as a whole. As a matter of fact, solutions for the principal problems of vaudeville came to us, so to speak, of themselves, during our work at the Artists' Theatre, so that we feel equipped and prepared for this project. Vaudeville, as it now stands—certainly its most skillful technical performances—should enjoy the position to which it is entitled, just as the theatre does. The technical performances of the vaudeville stage are always artistic in themselves. If they are not effective in present-day vaudeville shows, it is only because of tasteless make-up, bad costuming, and gaudy decoration. No uplift or education is necessary here; rather a tasteful treatment of such elegance as belongs to a proper vaudeville production.

And let us undertake this enterprise not just for the sake of vaudeville, but for the sake of the higher drama too. For the benefit of all theatrical art, it is necessary that we accept these artists as our friends. In such art circles, we shall find our most promising recruits. With their assistance we shall make more improvement in the players' craft than ever before, for most of these vaudeville productions demand, first of all, a perfectly healthy and beautifully developed body. They require an instinctive talent for controlling the body as a means of expression, for training it and making it supple and obedient to temperament, in short, everything that is known as a gymnastic education. We find such qualities among these younger variety artists far more than among the rising generation in the theatre. If one were to choose such individuals as in addition possess or can acquire the talents necessary for a musical education, one might hope to allay the heart-rending lamentations that all of the better theatrical producers raise over the lack of theatrical talent. The present situation is a sad one. The literary folk who are slaving away at the leading playhouses have little use for such primitive persons as vaudeville performers whose talent, exuberance, and animal spirits, impelled by a natural impulse to rhythmic expression, might make them creative artists. For the literati, the actor is merely a literary drudge.

With this suppression by literature of an entire class, the quality of theatrical aspirants sank also. This was only natural. So the prospect of working out really important theatrical problems became less and less likely for talented beginners. What literature demanded was more tricks of imitation. And even when literature called for the real creation of form, form nobly imagined and projected with integrity, the literary *régisseur* was likely to intervene with a demand for the differentiation of form, the projection of the merely accidental.

Therefore the more discriminating aspirants were glad to give up their theatrical careers, unless they had "voices" and so could become Wagnerian singers. No wonder that the supply of actors became poorer and poorer from year to year! With certain happy exceptions, the theatrical recruits of the literary era took on a decidedly plebeian character. Rickety, undernourished, or otherwise stunted types prevailed. Good extras are relatively plentiful, but well-bred types are wanting. Meanwhile, anyone with an eye trained in the plastic arts can see on the best stages, even through all the costuming, actresses whose appearance offends, heroes who waddle, heroines with hips deformed by stays, young lovers with paunches, and almost always, particularly among the younger performers, an amazing neglect of physical discipline. There is almost no evidence of good breeding, nor is there any sign of the general interest in sports which exists in Germany today. And why not? Because literature chooses its heroes from the "nobility" of the intellect: neurasthenics, hysterical persons, and other such patients of certain doctors and specialists. Why should beautiful, well-grown, fine-limbed, spirited people be attracted to the drama when it has become a psychological laboratory wherein he is most important who surrenders himself most readily as an experimental guinea pig to the research technicians investigating nervous diseases? How can one wonder at the poor quality of human stage material when the art of acting has been so ground into the dust by the tyranny of literature?

Go to the vaudeville houses! [1] There you will see "men who are men!" And marvelous women, too! There, everyone who has talent is given the opportunity to develop his ability without interference. Variety, therefore, offers much that is attractive both to strong animal natures and to the highest ranks of society, for in the highest social circles proficiency in sport sometimes gives its practitioners the quality of amateur vaudeville artists. Did not Goethe consider the physical beauty of men and women an essential factor in the artistic effect of the drama? While literary drama, continually favoring critical analysis, as is its way, lets bodily fitness languish on the stage, vaudeville offers unlimited scope to physical perfection and finds worthy recruits even among the very dregs of the proletariat. It attracts the most charming creatures, all kinds of colorful glittering figures, all sorts of surprising wonders. All the fresh, audacious boys and girls who have no money for an expensive education in the higher walks of the theatre find a home in vaudeville. And how many there are who if subjected to artistic influences would be capable of a greater degree of aesthetic development! In almost every vaudeville performance, even the most ordinary, one sees here a lad and there a girl of whom one may believe this and regret that so much natural talent should be wasted.

In order to gain experience in this field, we included a bill of Dance Fantasies ("*Tanzlegendchen*") in the repertoire of the Artists' Theatre. For the performance of the dances we chose only very youthful pupils, such ones from the ballet as had not lost their freshness in the routine. The results were successful beyond all expectation. Moreover, we had the satisfaction of seeing that the public, after it had overcome its first feeling of strangeness with regard to the new dramatic art form, plainly showed approval of the modest little offering. What we learned in this way prepares us to make, not only for the dance but for all kinds of vaudeville performances, the place in our cultural circles that belongs to them. To be sure, the requirements of variety call for something quite different from the amphitheatre. At vaudeville performances one wants to dine and drink, to chat and smoke, and one should be allowed to do so. The type of variety hall yet to be developed will combine the features of an elegant restaurant with those of a theatre with boxes. At any rate, we shall approach the solution of the cultural problem which vaudeville presents with the consciousness that it is no less worthy a task than that imposed by the drama and the opera.

VIII

The History of the Artists' Theatre

"DIE Sonne tönt nach alter Weise!" (The sun resounds as of old.) These were the first words that rang out from our new stage.

The Artists' Theatre grew out of a spirit of co-operation among the various practitioners of the plastic arts. This spirit was a vital force in the life of Munich. Here the consummation of such an enterprise was inevitable. But wherever in Germany such a stage might have developed, it would ultimately have had to prove its worth by a performance of Goethe's *Faust*. This was true not only because *Faust* is the greatest dramatic work in the German language but more especially because the first part of this tragedy conceals in its apparently chaotic structure more possibilities for the development of a dramatic style entirely independent of the ancient Latin examples than does any other classical work. As we can see today, there are in *Faust* the seeds of the future development of the German drama. And, because this powerful play forms a sort of threshold between the past and the future, it was inevitable that *Faust* should be used as the measure of any undertaking which aimed at the artistic development of the stage as a problem in design.

What would be gained by building a stage merely to suit this or that dramatic movement, as for instance the strictly classical style embodied in Schiller's *Braut von Messina*, or perhaps the undisciplined romantic style, or modern naturalism, or the even more modern new-romanticism? Such a stage might for the moment appear interesting or even sensational, but fundamentally it would be only an experiment in aesthetics without real value. It would disappear with the literary fashion which it served. But if one is to establish a stage which will serve a wide variety of dramatic forms, Goethe's *Faust* is the only prototype by which one may be guided, for this life-work of our greatest poet is the only drama that transcends all transient modes and embodies in its seemingly chaotic structure all possibilities of style.

This chaos in *Faust* is in reality a dramatic cosmos of meticulously organized technicalities. Its rhythm has not previously been appreciated because the play, when stretched upon the Procrustean bed of the opera stage, was torn limb from limb. Besides, we have been wrongly educated in the pedantic belief that the antique patterns, which since the time of Lessing and Schiller have been handed down to us in imitation of French classicism, were the only possible forms. Undoubtedly the style of the great court tragedies of Louis XIV was delicate, distinguished, and charming, qualities which we, as friends of Beardsley, would be the last to underestimate.

There is, however, in addition to the Greek and Latin style, another sort of stylization—one which has been notably developed in Germany. This fact is as true of the drama as it is of the plastic arts. Action in the geometric style of Aeschylus and Sophocles is built up with a triangular symmetry that recalls the decorative groupings in a classic pediment. This geometric style of classicism continued until Ibsen's time, and the construction of Ibsen's *Ghosts* is akin to that of Aeschylus' play *The Persians*. Lately, this form has been less esteemed. It has been the fashion to regard dramatic creations not as works of art to be appreciated and enjoyed for their artistic construction but rather as repositories of ethical codes, as tribunals of social criticism, as laboratories of applied psychology, or as showcases for the display of erotic curiosities.

The classic geometrical structure is in contrast to the more arithmetical style which was used by Shakespeare and later by Goethe in *Götz* and in *Faust*. Schiller also used it in *Die Räuber*. Such construction might be called the pictorial or graphic style. Here absolute symmetry is lacking. In such a design the rhythmic patterns are only discerned at a certain psychical distance, just as in looking at a picture one must step back from it in order to comprehend it and to appreciate its rhythmic unity. This sort of modern drama bears the same relationship to the antique drama as does an old German minster—one, of course, which has not been "restored!"—to the façade of an antique temple. The latter stands before us defined with uncompromising clarity, in a sharp and geometric unity of design. The cathedral with its Romanesque and Gothic windows, its baroque turrets, and its thousand and one additions only becomes comprehensible when we see it at a greater distance in relation to the whole town out of which it rises.

For this peculiarly modern style of drama which Goethe gave us in *Faust*, both classicism and naturalism were unsuitable. *Faust* was, therefore, considered undramatic—so much so that I was able to arrange for a production in the Munich Artists' Theatre only after considerable controversy.

Even in the inner circle of the Artists' Theatre there were not three people who had any faith in the success of *Faust;* in fact, vehement protests were registered against it. This was not surprising, for critics had long condemned *Faust* as drama because it was not didactically constructed according to plan F of some specific classical scheme. Directors and technicians had long ago ruined the play for the stage because by the use of excessive detail they had forced the spectators to focus their eyes, ears, and minds upon the play at as close range as though they were examining a miniature. In this way the impression of size and unity was lost.

For the appreciation of *Faust* the spectator should be conveyed to a great height from which the "chaos" will be seen to revolve about a focal point and so take on an inner meaning—just as the jumble of narrow streets, of roofs, angles, and courtyards together with the walls, spires, bridges, river, and outlying fields of an old town, when seen from a height, suddenly appear as an articulated unit governed by an individual and unmistakable rhythm which makes of churches, towers, and market place an organized whole. As the most perfect example of this more modern sort of dramatic rhythm, *Faust* was ideally constructed to furnish inspiration for an artistic and practical stage form; and through the exalted and vigorous imagination of Fritz Erler it became so. The stage of the Artists' Theatre was developed for the production of *Faust*, and therefore Goethe's work experienced there for the first time the success that it deserves. Everyone felt the force of its heightened dramatic impact.

I have frequently been asked how it happened that I began to think about a problem which at the time did not even seem to exist. No one worried about the level of taste in the conventional theatre. The fashionable literati were more than happy that the stage was copying nature, if only in cardboard. Discriminating people had long since ceased to attend the theatre, or, if they went, they had no respect for what they found there. In the circles in which I moved and in all the artistic life of Munich, no one thought of the theatre as an art equal to painting, music, architecture, or poetry, or expected of it such perfection as was required of the other arts. The theatre had grown out of the activities of wandering troupes; it would remain upon that level and would never be anything better no matter how many brilliant people wrote pieces for it. Such was the universal opinion.

It was anticipated that the theatre would soon be submerged in a slough of bad taste, as had happened in England, or would deteriorate into trivial frivolity, as in France. "It is to be hoped that this will happen speedily," they said, "so that we may start afresh. It is unfortunate to have a cultural activity of that kind continue; to have such egregious trash labeled as 'art' and set before the unsuspecting public with official sanction, with indeed the highest sanctions, only to ruin its taste." The repudiation of the theatre had become the order of the day, and those who felt about it in this way were the very people on whom its future depended, the people who in every other art had assumed responsibility for the cultural fortunes of Germany.

If I had not myself been a dramatist, I should never have relinquished this point of view which I shared completely. But from my own productions I was forced to realize that if we abandoned the theatre, we should destroy the art of dramatic poetry. That which we had dreamed of in our youthful naïveté had proved to be childish nonsense. We had believed that we could renounce the theatre of tradition and conjure a "theatre of culture" out of the air. As I followed the cultural movement which developed under the designation of applied art, I came to see the true state of affairs. I saw how the most distinguished of the younger generation of artists, having wearied of creating pictures and statues for which there was no place in the cultural life of the present, set to work to influence that life, to improve the means of production, and to create a world of good taste in which their pictures and statues would again be esteemed as useful and necessary.

The creation of works of art solely for galleries and museums, which was previously recommended to workers in the plastic arts, corresponds to the creation of drama which, being buried in books and libraries, fails of its purpose. Our friends in the plastic arts struggled against a world of prejudice. There was not the slightest indication of a crying need among the educated public for sound standards in the field of decoration, for better means of production, or for decent domestic architecture. In the same way dramatic art was forced to develop a culture for the stage and raise the theatre to its own level instead of waiting until the theatre could drag itself out of the general confusion. We had helped our friends in the plastic arts to realize their plans; it was quite natural now that they should make common cause with us, for fundamentally we had the same goal.

Soon after the appearance of the first statement by which I endeavored to win favor for these ideas, a sort of concentration of cultural forces seemed to set in. The Grand Duke of Hesse founded the artists' colony at Darmstadt. I laid before the Grand Duke a memorandum which coincided with his own enthusiastic determination to bring the problem of the rehabilitation of the stage to the attention of the company of artists around him. Of these artists it was particularly Peter Behrens who recognized at once that here was a task for the accomplishment of which the aid of the architect and the designer was needed.

It soon became apparent that a compromise with existing conditions would be foolish, for the existing conditions were not the result of a continuation of traditional forms. Behrens set to work at once on the whole problem. He supplied both architectural plans and literary articles so that, when the preparations for the Darmstadt Exposition of 1901 were begun, we had made sufficient progress to think we might exhibit a small stage as a sort of model of the type of theatre which we expected to perfect. The work had progressed very well, and even the program of plays was, in the main, arranged. But shortly before the opening of the Exposition we decided that to hurry such an important venture might do more harm than good. The affair could only prosper if we were able not only to expound a principle but to make a demonstration that would be completely convincing. In no other way could we advance dramatic art as a whole toward the proper sort of theatre. Such a demonstration could not be accomplished in Darmstadt in the time available and with the materials at hand. So we renounced the easy pleasure of a speedy and sensational success and resigned the space to other uses. But we were conscious that our work had not been in vain.

We had finally brought the question under discussion, and it could not be dropped until it had been answered. Also—and this was perhaps more important—we had discovered certain essential things about the reform movements in German theatrical history of the nineteenth century, things which for the most part had been forgotten or misunderstood. In my pamphlet of 1900 the heart of the matter was set forth in these words:

The great activity in applied art and decoration is encouraging, and it gives us the very tools we need with which to rebuild the German stage in a modern form and spirit. . . . In the works of the distinguished painters, sculptors, and decorators of our time there are infinite resources which have never been made use of by that very art which exercises the most direct and comprehensive influence on cultivated people. To claim these resources for the stage it is only necessary, with the help of our artists, to produce plays in such a way as to inspire artistic appreciation.

In keeping with the spirit of modern applied art, stage design should be based on the functional requirements of the theatre, not upon abstract theories of aesthetics, not upon historical erudition nor upon pleasure in the reproduction of antiquity. Everything should be simple as to color, line, and architecture. The drama should be apprehended by the artist in a personal way and from its inception so planned that the play and the performers may achieve a purer and more powerful effect than was formerly thought possible.

This program differentiated us sharply from all reformers, since we were determined to build in a new and fundamental fashion. It separated us most sharply from the Meiningen Theatre. The same unbridgeable chasm which divides Leibl from Piloty, which differentiates the Renaissance style from modern applied art, separates the Munich Artists' Theatre from the Meiningen school. This is true in spite of the fact that in Bayreuth the Meiningen techniques were expertly developed. It is still true even when, by the genius of Max Reinhardt, these techniques have been made appetizing enough for the most refined taste. Our philosophy was quite different. The Artists' Theatre has no more in common with the various sorts of stage reforms than modern applied art has with reforms of industrial art.

To be sure, a sharp reaction against the reign of Meiningen had set in a generation earlier. The principles of the Meiningen school, principles of noble origin, had been unscrupulously exploited. Odious ostentation, scholastic pedantry, and the bombastic acting of an earlier age were by-products of the Meiningen stage. Plays and performers sank beneath the burden of this egregious rubbish. They grimaced and cavorted; with ranting and roaring they overacted. Things came to such a pass that, although this was an era in which taste was universally debased, the stage stood upon the very lowest level of degradation.

It is no wonder that the resulting reaction was so severe, as, for example, in the case of the Munich Shakespeare Stage with its puritanical austerity. Nevertheless, this movement will one day be listed at the head of an important chapter of German theatrical history as the first decisive symptom of the recovery of the German stage, and its leaders will be accorded places of distinction. That the Munich Shakespeare Stage was discontinued was not the fault of the highminded men who co-operated in the endeavor. The fault lay in the condition of the times. It was not until the next generation that designers appeared who were equal to such a task and who were objective enough in thought to subordinate decoration, painting, and design to the functions of the drama.

It was obvious, even then, that the problem could not be solved without designers. No director, not even the greatest genius; no technician, not even the most resourceful, can be expected to create an artistic arrangement of space such as the stage requires—an arrangement whereby the dramatic action and its vehicle, the performer, may appear in that particular relationship to the spectator which we consider artistic and in the artistic sense true and convincing. This is a problem for the architect and the designer. In this period there were no designers of this caliber. The architects only drew façades, and the painters and other workers merely occupied themselves with decoration. They were happiest when they could smother everything under reproductions of authentic styles. If at this time there had been designers with an understanding of the problem and if they had been called in to assist in the stage reform, they would have instantly understood that stage and auditorium are an organic whole. They would have bridged the gap which divided stage and amphitheatre just as several decades earlier Semper,[1] the creator of the Wagnerian amphitheatre,[2] longed to do. But unfortunately a man like Semper did not then exist.

The principles of design which govern the stage are dependent on certain definite optical and acoustical relationships with the auditorium. Since the originators of the Shakespeare Stage were forced to ignore the auditorium, they were prevented from carrying out these principles. The result was that the performers, as well as the artists, were thwarted in the development of their creative potentialities. Nevertheless, the experiment was in itself such a great gain that those connected with the Shakespeare Stage should be mentioned with honor and with gratitude, especially by us, since we can by no means claim to have solved the problem in all its details.

In Munich a comradeship between drama and the fine arts, which facilitates the solution of theatrical problems, has always existed. Indeed the temper of Munich is such that the theatre cannot be accepted there on any other terms. When in my article of November 10, 1904, in the *Neuer Verein,* I developed the principles of such a synthesis, I met with the heartiest agreement among the leading personalities in fine and applied art. One man whose collaboration was of paramount importance presented himself at this time desiring to be of service. This man was Max Littmann. He put at the disposal of the undertaking an incomparable fund of experience in theatre building, a wealth of architectural skill, and a rare talent for organization. As an authority on the work of the master builders Schinkel and Semper, who several decades before had striven for the same goals, he also brought us into closer contact with tradition.*

As a result we have gradually discovered a series of remarkable circumstances which prove to us with absolute certainty that Goethe, Schiller, Schinkel—in short, all the leading spirits of the generation under whose supervision the rise of the German drama took place—tried to inaugurate exactly the same sort of staging which we are endeavoring to establish. It was only because of the excessive growth of the Italian opera, because of the coupling of opera and play in many of the large theatres, and because of other untoward circumstances that their plans were shattered and finally forgotten. Thus we came into possession of a noble heritage! We were in the same situation as the representatives of applied art and of modern architecture who, at the moment when they fought their way to freedom, realized that what they had been working toward was actually a restoration of the sound practices which had existed before the onset of that era which had demoralized all conceptions of style. We found that our task was the same as theirs, namely, to make serviceable to our uses those powerful adjuncts which modern technology had been developing in the meantime.

To this end, practical experiments were indispensable. In his paper on the Schiller Theatre, which he built at Charlottanburg, Littmann describes the course of the experiments which took place in the spring of 1906 in the

* The historical documents have been printed in the official records of the Munich Artists' Theatre published by Georg Müller, page 35.

Prince Regent Theatre in Munich. They had to do with determining the manner in which a proscenium should be constructed in order to assure the proper relationship between stage and auditorium. Moreover, they had to do with the improvement of stage lighting. For the time being, scene design and decoration were not considered, since the gigantic stage of the Prince Regent Theatre is arranged for the Wagnerian music drama.

Here, on the fifteenth of May, 1906, there took place on an experimental stage constructed by Littmann a performance of my play *Till Eulenspiegel*. Perhaps no drama ever had a more precarious tryout than on this makeshift stage, which was half the old-fashioned peep-show, wing stage of grand opera, and half the partially developed relief stage of the future. Although under these ambiguous conditions the players as well as the public were confused, we were nevertheless encouraged to the further development of our ideas.

We discovered from the results of our tryouts in the Prince Regent Theatre exactly how the house, proscenium, stage, lighting, and equipment ought to be arranged. The next thing was to solve the problems of scenic architecture together with all the related artistic problems of decoration and costume. For this it was necessary to approach a wider artistic circle—persons who were authorities on painting, sculpture, decoration, and costume design.

Accordingly, it became my task to convince the leading spirits in the fine arts that the stage might properly participate in the cultural development in which we were all taking part and to assure them that their creative powers would not be exploited for the purpose of patching up the conventional theatre and the literary drama but that an organic change in the theatre might actually be achieved.

It was years before our artists considered it possible to make the theatre what they called "decently artistic," though the vaudeville stage had long since won their warmest approval. Their aversion was not merely to the arrangement and decoration of the scenes and to the ostentation and deception of the construction but to the ridiculous pomposity of the literati. This painters found especially offensive, since they had but recently freed themselves from literature by a bitterly fought revolution. Much of this aversion, in fact most of it, was justified. But much was also founded on prejudice.

It was therefore fortunate that I was successful in winning over a painter who, more than any other man, possessed the full confidence of all the workers in the fine arts. And when the storm of opinions has subsided, and critics have recognized that the Artists' Theatre has contributed lasting and valuable inspiration to the development of the stage, the name of Benno Becker will be written in large letters in this chapter of German theatrical history. It is seldom that one finds a man in whom the human and artistic characteristics necessary for such a comprehensive piece of organization are united in such measure and who is ready to dedicate himself so unselfishly to a good cause.

It was also fortunate that the director of the Munich branch of the Dresden Bank, Wilhelm Seitz, the same financier who first made it possible for applied art to become a successful business enterprise, also created a sound financial foundation for the Artists' Theatre. In this he was supported by Consul Heinrich Roeckl, who had already proved himself a good adviser of the Munich artists in other undertakings, and by Dr. Wilhelm Rosenthal, who as president of the *Neuer Verein* had rendered lasting services to the advancement of dramatic art in Munich.

The directors and councilors who met under the leadership of His Excellency Ceremonialmaster Count Max von Moy drew up a concise program. Many of these prominent men did not feel themselves restricted by their membership on this committee from expressing themselves in other ways for the good of the cause and co-operated in an effective way in the artistic organization, particularly Adolf von Hildebrand, Toni Stradler, Richard Riemerschmid, II, Georg Kerschensteiner, the gifted organizer of our educational system, and the authors Paul Marsop, Georg Schaumberg, Leo Greiner, and others.

Ever since the days of King Ludwig I, the city of Munich has pioneered both in the development of the German stage and in the progress of plastic art. The leading spirits of Munich have always debated the possibility of an amalgamation of these two areas of endeavor. When the realization of this dream was at hand, it was consistent with tradition that the undertaking should come under the patronage of the House of Wittelsbach. Prince Rupprecht of Bavaria appeared as head of the movement. It was also appropriate that the Artists' Theatre should be located on the Theresienhöhe beside the monument of Ludwig I which overlooks Schwanthaler's statue of *Bavaria*.

There this project of the city of Munich was begun in that quiet forest, the Exposition Park, which had been planted by the artist king. What Devrient prophesied has actually come to pass—the artists and citizens of Munich have come together under the egis of the House of Wittelsbach to inaugurate an artists' theatre for Germany.

But the idea would have been difficult to develop without the assistance of the head of the Bavarian Court Theatre, Excellenz von Speidel, who immediately recognized its potential value. Nevertheless, the co-operation of the Artists' Theatre and. the Munich Court Theatre presented certain problems. The Court Theatre in Munich had for years been so neglected in favor of Wagnerian opera that it was almost forgotten by many of the people who would otherwise have been its ardent supporters. The literary trend of the drama found few adherents in Munich after the period of the Ibsen influence had declined. Therefore the idea of co-operation with the Court Theatre was declared to be inadvisable—particularly by those people who admitted that they had not seen a performance at the Court Theatre for years!

And so I began to study the theatrical situation and conscientiously to attend productions, even the most antiquated classical performances. At these I found only high school boys and boarding school girls with a few candy-nibbling elderly females and pathetic governesses such as were using up their subscription seats and stoically struggling to comprehend interpretations of classic characters which had not the remotest connection with life.

I decided that it was only necessary to break through the shell of tradition to discover here the same talents which were present during the generation of Dahn, Hausmann, Keppler, Häusser, and Suske. Accordingly, I proposed the consolidation of the Artists' Theatre and the Court Theatre, and I have never regretted it. One of the biggest surprises that the Artists' Theatre brought was the sudden appearance on the stage of the Court Theatre of talents which, under ordinary circumstances, would never have shown up. This, however, is actually not so surprising. For as soon as one creates the proper relationship between the scene and the spectator, not only are the strengths of the actor revealed, but his weaknesses are exposed also. Therefore he is compelled to exert himself more intensively to, as they say, "put himself into the part."

Our actors have generally found this agreeable, once they have become accustomed to the new conditions. And there has grown up between the actors and the workers in plastic art a mutual confidence and a recognition of their interdependence. The designer needs the co-operation of the performers if he is to create costumes and scenery to suit their work. Therefore performer and designer must understand each other. It is an outstanding artistic achievement on the part of the Munich Court Theatre to have shown that such co-operation is possible. On this foundation theatrical accomplishments of the future will so develop as to become an organic part of our civilization.

IX

The New Art of the Stage and the Commercial Theatre

FROM all over Europe and from the United States people have come to Munich and have studied our plant. Many crawled into the darkest corners to make sure that no screw or lever escaped them. Such over-zealous investigations were of course quite pointless. The theatre has again become an art, and only those who regard it in this way will be able to work effectively in the spirit of the Artists' Theatre. It is a mistake to believe that plastic art and the new theatrical techniques which have developed out of it can be used to embellish the literary drama and the explicitly untheatrical manner of presentation which is indigenous to it. Such exertions would be futile. The activities of the Artists' Theatre have value only if they lead to a revolt that works outward from within.

I suspect that in certain quarters the Artists' Theatre

will be mistakenly acclaimed as a new fashion; and I foresee that certain theatrical directors will be chagrined to discover that the popularity which they had hoped to achieve by following this fashion does not materialize.

Also, they may try to produce more cheaply. Instead of using established artists of distinction, they may call on more modest talent, or on clever beginners in search of a reputation. In this case we shall see a sort of theatrical "youth movement." The old, conventional crudenesses will reappear in newfangled disguises. Theatrical workers will occupy themselves with modes of decoration until this phase too has been exhausted. One disappointment will follow another wherever the heart of the matter is not resolutely adhered to, that is, wherever we fail to follow that artistic spirit which builds from within outward, which evolves from the dramatic situation the scene, from the scene the stage, from the stage the house, and everything else that we need for the enjoyment of the theatrical experience. So the new Festival House on the Theresienhöhe must for years to come create new artistic forms with new materials before the real character of the undertaking is everywhere apprehended and esteemed.

The essential thing is not that one stylize stage, scene, and costumes in this or that manner. The essential thing is that once more there shall be plays in the playhouses. The leading modern houses in the big cities, which for the sake of literature neglected the principles of art, are being ruined. The literary cliques, after the fashion of all promotors of organized mediocrity, gain control of the directors by offering them personal publicity and financial assistance, and then, fearful of competition, allow no superior talent or genuine theatrical capacity to appear among the novices. Importation brings only stale wares, and infinite boredom soon yawns on all sides. To be sure, the general hopelessness is sometimes relieved by sound theatrical practice in an occasional Shakespearian performance, such as Max Reinhardt's overwhelmingly theatrical production of *As You Like It.*

Until such time as the established theatres learn to foster a type of dramatic production which is as genuinely theatrical as it is authentically artistic and sincerely poetic, it will be all the more imperative for the truly theatrical art form to be certain of an assured place at least in the Festival House.

As to the drama in the court theatres and in the theatres of the larger cities, the imposition of literary standards during the middle of the last century set them an impossible task, namely, that of giving an historical survey of literature. The new political factions which were just coming into power sponsored this apparently public-spirited project. Under constitutional government, the court theatres lost their original character as places of purely courtly entertainment. The treasuries had to be filled by the taxpayers, and it was the community that now subsidized the theatres. Therefore, the taxpayers or their chosen representatives (in certain cases "public opinion" as represented by the literary critics) were justified in claiming the right to exert an influence on the theatrical profession.

As far as the opera is concerned, the *bourgeoisie* made decidedly productive use of its influence in artistic matters, thus proving the high level to which music had attained as the only really popular art in Germany. The opera rose to unprecedented heights and, even in the rendering of the great classic masters, soon surpassed the courtly era. But the new conditions affected the drama in the court theatres and in the theatres of the larger cities which copied the court theatres in a very different way from that in which they affected the opera.

In court society of an earlier epoch the qualities of art and taste were the deciding factors with regard to the drama. A good performance was demanded, and literary considerations never entered in. If one talked to the clever, cultivated old men and women who as the last survivors of the "good old days" were able to tell about the theatre, they always discussed the quality of the *actors* who had received the "Bravos" of that era, and they mentioned the plays only in passing. Even the first performances of certain classics which they had attended in the little court theatres they so passionately adored: these, too, were forgotten. One asked in vain concerning the impression made by the first presentation of *Götz*, or *Wallenstein*. One inquired fruitlessly concerning a certain production of Shakespeare, or even concerning the effect of *Faust* upon its original audience. But one was showered with enthusiastic and affecting reminiscences of the "superb" playing of some individual performer, regardless of whether he appeared in a role in some long-forgotten piece of Kotzebue, or Iffland, or Houwald, or even of Birch-Pfeiffer, or whether he played in some classic masterpiece which was subsequently canonized. Only in Weimar, where the poets themselves were personally known and where they actually participated in their own productions, may the situation have been somewhat different.

The bourgeois audiences of the middle of the past century, however, lacked the capacity for such enjoyment of the art of acting. This is not surprising, for the more distinguished theatres tolerated the simple burgher only as a groundling in the pit, and he had as little opportunity to improve his understanding of the art of acting as he had to study good pictures and learn to appreciate quality in painting. The new society was interested only in scientific culture, and this fact also influenced the theatre. If a play was to be more than mere amusement, if it was to receive public support, it must make itself useful by dispensing knowledge of literary culture and by contributing to the moral education of the people and particularly to the "development of youth." The court theatre became a factor in the scheme of public education and culture and was forced, in the fulfillment of its civic duties, to make an "established classical repertory" part of its working plan.

This is what brought about the slow but certain death of dramatic art and the art of acting in these theatres, for it is quite impossible for a classical repertory to be successfully maintained, even according to the most modest artistic standards, when it must contain the best works of Shakespeare, Calderón, Molière, Lessing, Schiller, Goethe, Kleist, Hebbel, and so many others whose works have been raised to the rank of classics. This historical survey of literature could only be furnished when director and actors accustomed themselves to work with patterns that had been crudely cut out and that were applied to everything. What was thought right for the classicists was considered fair enough for other authors also. The art of acting stiffened into mannerisms which even an actor of genius was powerless to change once the theatrical dictators had fitted him into the mold of the theatre as an actor of this or that type.

It is unnecessary to describe the sort of routine that set in. Everyone knows about it, and everyone knows the results: the best elements in the tradition of the art of acting were lost and the classical drama was destroyed. In the consciousness of cultivated people such plays were in the same category with the emphasis on Latin grammar which, on account of the dogmatic practices of the classroom, made the beauty of the ancient poets distasteful to us.

Today the court theatres must play their obligatory classical performances at reduced prices in order to get any audiences at all. Even the most highly educated, who by their own endeavors have discovered the inner significance of the classics, even they do not go to see classical plays performed because they know better than anyone else that the cut-and-dried performances of the last fifty years gave a completely false idea of classical drama.

By the same token, the new naturalism of the eighties and nineties—in spite of its basically childish and dilettante conception—found a public during this period. These tiresome, bungling performances, ugly and painful as they often were, were nevertheless departures from the stereotyped pattern. And therefore, in spite of their uninspired, moralizing pedantry, they were welcome to the young and talented actors who longed for change, because they recognized in them a new task which gave them a chance for original creative work.

Forthwith, the "classical repertoire," that pride of the nation, was buried. The intellectual and cultural element threw itself feverishly into the pursuit of this "naturalism," as did the new acting talent. And the result is that today in the younger generation of actors the types necessary for the classic repertory are entirely lacking. Soon there will be no more "heroes" and no more "heroines." Even the great character actors are dying out, and—what is still more amazing—even the comedians!

One discovers that an astonishing situation exists in the detheatricalized theatre of today when one evaluates it as a cultural institution. The art of acting and repertoire both are bankrupt! No one goes to see productions of the classics once he has outgrown the compulsion of his school days. And if here and there a significant performer or an outstanding director, such as Max Reinhardt, did not by his individual competence prove to us the immortal vitality of the old masters, the casual public would be right in thinking that the classical authors, even Shakespeare, had long since been discarded.

Such things happen when art is used for inartistic purposes. Evil rather than good is bound to result. So long as this dead weight is not lifted from the court theatres, most of them, in so far as the drama is concerned, will not be able to recover. They will be doomed to financial failure, and so the state treasury as well as the support of royalty will be uselessly sacrificed. The classics will not have been brought nearer to the people and to the rising generation, but more removed from them. No theatre in the world, not even the best conducted and best accoutred, can put on an established classical repertoire in such a manner that the individual pieces will be lively and convincing. Foolish, inartistic things have been asked of the theatre, and it is not surprising that a crisis threatens.

In the court theatres and the theatres of the larger cities, action must be directed particularly against this kind of literary peonage, against the established classical repertory and its aftereffects. Here too, commercial considerations hasten the inevitable crisis. That the crisis has not yet set in is only because in none of the principalities has a ruler arisen who has had the same regard for the drama that some have had for architecture, for applied art, or for the opera. The younger German rulers have had the same attitude toward the theatre as the rest of the younger generation in Germany; the presentations of the classics and the sterile period of naturalism banished the drama from their horizon. In the assemblies of the several different states there was not a single outstanding personality with sufficient interest in the drama to note the fact that, even from a business point of view, things were not as they should be.

A reaction is inevitable. In the Artists' Theatre it has been shown that it is quite possible to run the business of a court theatre in a highly profitable manner. Not by concessions in favor of that which is banal or in bad taste, but by working out the plays of the old masters in such an artistic way that their fire consumes the trite patterns and inflames our hearts anew. If during a year a theatre puts on only one or two effective masterpieces, such as the production of *Faust* as performed by the members of the Munich Court Theatre at the Artists' Theatre, it accomplishes more for artistic, literary, and ethical education than an established classical repertoire of a hundred pieces, all of which fall short of their effect because of the hackneyed manner of their presentation.

We are faced with a situation similar to that which existed in the management of our art galleries. These too were once thought to be most helpful in the education of youth and of the masses if they were hung full of pictures which, by their historical significance, their literary spirit, and moral content, taught "lessons of wisdom and virtue." Today we see that the millions spent for such stupid things was money thrown away and that, moreover, the development of painting in Germany under this system of literary galleries has suffered greatly.

As these once revered historical atrocities in their fat gold frames now hang covered with dust and cobwebs on the back stairways of our renovated galleries and museums, so the classics hang today in the repertoires of our official theatres. There are court theatres that present *Faust*, the *Wallenstein Trilogy*, and other such stock pieces in exactly the same fashion as they did in the year one. In the thirties, forties, and fifties, or at latest in the eighties and nineties, that is, in a tasteless and obsolete period, these roles were first "created," and they have never been thoroughly worked on since then. All that has been done has been to give each newly engaged performer a few hurried rehearsals in the same old techniques. In this manner, whole generations of actors have been poured into the same moulds—new wine into fifty-year-old bottles.

If the people in authority at the courts and in the various states and cities of Germany were finally to decide to go themselves to see such a presentation of the classics, instead of sending half-grown children and their nurses, they would have their eyes opened as to the causes of financial distress in the playhouses. The Artists' Theatre has proved that the classics can be given in such a way as to make them even more attractive to the public than are the silly hits-of-the-season with which such playhouses usually keep their heads above water.

There will always be poor theatres, and these may always be in the majority and have the largest attendance when they cater to the vulgar instincts of the masses, among the rich as well as the poor. But eventually the heads of the large theatres which are supported by public funds will be chosen by the same standards as those now used in choosing directors for art schools and selecting the superintendents of other cultural institutions. Important theatres will not be handed over to contending tradesmen, or to conscientious but inwardly unsympathetic administrative officials, or to imposing commissions holding a chance political majority. Neither will they be handed over to the servants of the literary cliques, or to the impeccable gentlemen behind the green-topped table; least of all to the unscrupulous lessees who, after they have enriched themselves, leave to an impoverished government a theatre artistically and financially mismanaged and a public completely demoralized. To fill these positions, the incumbents of which mould the public taste, a search will be made for outstanding personalities in the great stream of our cultural renaissance. Nor will their cultural pre-eminence prevent them from being good businessmen. On the contrary, they will take all the more pains with the financial organization because they will be conscious that they represent large and important interests, which they will not dare expose to any risk.[1]

The careful conduct of the business aspects of the Artists' Theatre may be traced to such considerations. We held it to be our duty to prove that even the financial matters of a theatre are nowhere better tended than by men who are most seriously interested in art. This demonstration was made under difficult circumstances. There were only six hundred seats to be sold, the price of tickets was augmented by the entrance fee to the Exposition, and the enormous initial expenditure had to be paid off during a five-month playing time. The demonstration was so successful that all doubts were silenced. Perhaps in this one fact we may see the most notable achievement of the Artists' Theatre, for, if the court councils and city administrations will draw from this fact the obvious lesson and from now on place outstanding personalities of creative bent at the head of theatres, everything else will turn out well.

Then it will be understood that this movement, which is now considered revolutionary, is merely the renascence of a sound inheritance after a period of chaos which was at variance with our best traditions.

Appendix

It is not fitting that I, who am so vitally concerned, should pass judgment on the results of the Artists' Theatre. But since it is important that various points of view be expressed, I have decided to follow my discussion with extracts from the opinions of leading critics and newspapers. I have indeed been forced to this by the circulation of certain statements calculated to confuse the situation. One falsehood, for example, which was continually recurrent and therefore malicious was the statement that the Artists' Theatre was a theatrical movement directed against Brahm and Reinhardt. In the first place, the Artists' Theatre was in no wise a "theatrical movement" but rather a voluntary consolidation of the plastic artists of Munich with the Court Theatre in order that, in the auditorium which had already been erected on the exposition grounds, they might attempt the solution of certain definite theatrical problems which, within the confines of the existing theatrical industry, were unfortunately not to be solved. Furthermore, there could be no opposition to Brahm and Reinhardt since these managers could nowhere have found warmer recognition of their aspirations and accomplishments than in that circle in which the Artists' Theatre originated. Moreover, both Brahm and Reinhardt showed sympathetic understanding of the aims of the Artists' Theatre, subscribed, indeed, to the undertaking, and accepted the results in principle. We felt that we represented a cause undertaken in behalf of *all* serious-minded, artistically inclined theatrical managers. We have extended the most cordial welcome to all representatives of any branch of the theatre desiring to become acquainted with our devices and to make use of our discoveries, for our undertaking was not in competition with the existing theatres but was intended to be to their advantage.

The following criticisms,[1] therefore, are only meant to show how far, in the estimation of established critics, the embodiment of our principles has been successful and what benefits may be expected from them for the advancement of the theatre.

New Yorker Staatszeitung (New York), May 24, 1908:

In another part of this paper, among the art notes cabled from Berlin, our readers will learn that the Artists' Theatre,

[1] *Die Revolution des Theaters* contains some fifty contemporary reviews from newspapers and periodicals, almost all of them favorable. The ten that are included here have been chosen because they represent a number of different nationalities and geographical locations, because they give especially vivid descriptions of the productions that they review, or because they indicate significant contemporary reactions to the enterprise.

an attraction of the present exposition at Munich, has aroused much interest with a performance of *Faust*. Otto Julius Bierbaum in a Berlin paper tells us something about this venture of Georg Fuchs, concerning the aim and purpose of which so little has thus far reached us from across the ocean.

We do not yet know how it will materialize, but one may have the highest expectations. I formed such expectations on reading the advance notices in the article published in Berlin in which the Munich Artists' Theatre set forth its program. This program will commence at the beginning of the Exposition, but the theatre will continue to be useful far beyond the duration of the Exposition. It will exemplify ideas which, no matter how they may turn out during this first attempted realization, will certainly not be without influence in the life of our theatre. Perhaps (and we may hope) these ideas may even bring about a new era in German theatrical history. When I first heard of them I had the impression they were for the advantage of certain playwrights who were unable to meet the requirements of the existing stage, and who hoped to achieve their goal on a new stage where plastic art would serve to supply the deficiencies left by their lack of skill in the use of the spoken word. And I feared that, in addition to the impetus given to these intrinsically undramatic talents, there would be an overemphasis on such arts as please the eye but defeat the drama. Instead, I find, to my great joy, that the Munich program possesses a true dramatic spirit which makes quite clear in what order the arts of the theatre are to function.

It is also quite evident that this undertaking will be a great experience for all those who in any way have—or would like to have—a connection with the theatre. For Herr Fuchs is surely right when he maintains that aesthetically fastidious circles of society must be won back to the theatre—those people who, according to Count Kessler, shun the theatre. Even if this attempt, which has been undertaken with so much spirit and understanding, should fail entirely (which I do not believe) no one connected with it will have wasted his time. For it will be the token of a cultural and aesthetic *tour de force* such as people of today are seldom privileged to see. Never has an exposition had such a significant attraction. May it outlast this exposition as did the Eiffel Tower, which from an exposition exhibit became one of the world's monuments.

Neue Züricher Zeitung (Zurich), May 28, 1908:

There is today a certain attitude toward the theatre as though it were a sort of *mauvais sujet*, with which a person of sensibility and cultivation should avoid all contact. And yet experience teaches us that there is nothing in which the general public has more interest than the theatre.

The unusually audacious experiment of the Artists' Theatre began with an artistic re-creation of Goethe's *Faust* by Fritz Erler, which might almost be called revolutionary. It made, judging by the first performance, a very strong impression. Everyone had the feeling that he was present at a significant, perhaps even an epoch-making, event. One cannot, however, say whether or not *Faust* in the form in which we now behold it at the Artists' Theatre will sooner or later become the common property of the German stage. Probably not. Reviewing it all briefly one might say: That which Fritz Erler has accomplished is a work of art of the very greatest importance, the absolute worth of which even the opponents of the experiment must admit.

R. B.

Chronicle of the Arts (Paris), May 20, 1908:

On Sunday May 17, the Artists' Theatre,—which is supposed to be the center of the Jubilee Exposition at Munich and is indeed its chief attraction—opened its doors for a gala presentation of Goethe's *Faust*. An amazing effect was produced by the spirited scenery of Fritz Erler combined with the evocative music of Max Schilling. Erler, whose frescoes at Wiesbaden have won him a celebrity which borders almost on the scandalous, has just acquired substantial fame through his decorations for *Faust.* They constitute a veritable revolution in scenic art, and the theatres throughout Germany will doubtless accept these principles of simplification. These have to do with the substitution of genuine design for the more or less successful visual deception which has heretofore been called decoration. He uses a system of three movable pieces, two vertical and one horizontal (sometimes raised and sometimes lowered), related to the wings and capable of serving as the bases for any sort of scenic decoration, hence serving better than wings in representing on the shallowest stage the most ambitious dramas of Goethe and Shakespeare, which are usually the most mangled, and of doing so without waits of more than two or three minutes, often only the time it takes to drop the curtain. For example, the horizontal piece, when lowered, marks the line of march along which the Easter Promenade unrolls like a frieze. On it stand the three imposing archangels of the prologue in Heaven. Raised, it forms a long wall (in the third scene from the last: a dark day on the heath) from the top of which the arrogant Mephisto scornfully contemplates the suppliant Faust begging to be led back to Marguerite. The two vertical pieces, more or less separated, suffice for all the various streets, squares, cathedrals, and outdoor scenes, and when combined with the horizontal pieces, for all the interiors and for the scene in the garden. We have only to add a frieze to diminish the height ad libitum. It is a veritable egg of Columbus!

The elements which contribute to this amazingly unpretentious scheme for producing scenic illusion are simplicity itself, but they are combined with such intelligence as to result in clear pictures in which everything contributes to the action and nothing detracts from it. Faust's armchair turned about becomes that of Marguerite within the embrasure of her window, and this embrasure becomes the background in the scene in which the gossips taunt her. Alongside this is placed the Mater Dolorosa, and thus an entr'acte is abolished. The stairs which descend into Auerbach's tavern and the tavern itself, with the use of altered lighting and the minimum of modification becomes the prison in the last scene. Obviously light is an important factor. The most powerful effects are attained by artifices which are, properly speaking, childishly simple, as the bouquets of red flowers in the garden of which one single flower, as night comes on, holds the light longer than the others. The presentation of Heaven, of Walpurgis Night, of the abode of the witches, are set forth so ingeniously, so convincingly, and so impressively that no other theatre, even one with the most costly and elaborate equipment, has ever equaled it. And the repeated and imaginative use of the same designs, the same patterns, as the scenes succeed one another contrives to give a feeling of unity to this disjointed drama, a sort of implacable unity which the eye imposes on the spirit.

Furthermore, in the Erler tableaus, these scenes are designed more beautifully than ever before. His method is to place the horizon line so low that most of the landscape lies behind the legs of the moving characters. So, in the out-of-door scenes the actors are silhouetted against the sky and so given much greater importance. In costume there is the same simplification, whether of realism, archaism, or local color. This play was only vaguely *moyen âge*. All the customary striving after exactitude is useless because it is continually frustrated by the accidental. On the other hand, we find repeatedly that the fresh arrangement of colors, the rehabilitation of disregarded harmonies, the reversal of the common implications of color values contribute to Mr. Erler's art. For example, for the drunken scene in the tavern immaculate white prevails.

Without prejudice against the four or five other painters,

each of whom is commissioned to produce a play according to his type, it is possible that the Erler *Faust* may be the most significant production of the Artists' Theatre. The opinion is unanimous among those who are interested that within a short time there will be a revolution in all the theatres of Germany.

WILLIAM RITTER

Stage Decoration (Paris), June 23, 1908:

It is now almost a month since the Exposition at Munich opened its doors. For today let us talk a bit about the outstanding feature of that exposition, the little artists' theatre, a veritable jewel of good taste, which connoisseurs consider an important step in the evolution of theatrical art and of scenic decoration in particular.

At the time of the antique tragedies and of Shakespeare's dramas what we call stage decoration was ignored. One set without decoration, a simple platform where the actors recited their roles—this was the only frame for the dramatic action. So that, deprived of all exterior artifice, the player was obliged to capture the interest of the spectators solely by his own intensity. . . . Later, in French tragedy, it was the beauty of the discourse and the harmony brought about by the strict observance of the rules of unity that made for success. After a time the painted backdrop was imported from Italy. Then one sees that, after having been for some time quite unrelated to the play, the scenery became more specialized and more complicated. For this type of decoration scenery of the classical epoch represented now a palace, now an interior, now a public place, and served as desired for diverse sorts of plays. Then came first the romantic setting of Hugo and Sardou, with its pretentious and surprising picturesque effects, and finally naturalism with its meticulous attention to detail.

That is where we are at present. An interest in stage decoration too often encroaches upon the interest in dramatic action.

And this progressive evolution has been in part disastrous. The essence of a drama is in its action. Everything that detracts from the immediate effect should be considered harmful. The scenic effect should serve only to heighten the dramatic impression, and for this reason it is necessary that it remain subordinated to the action, of which it is only the frame.

To give to the dramatic work all its rightful importance by surrounding it with a suitable decoration, artistically adapted to the effect of the whole, this is the undertaking which has been carried out with great success by the Artists' Theatre at Munich.

I attended with astonishment the presentation of an exquisite Shakespearian comedy. What a splendid and spirited impression was here created, thanks to the co-operation of decorative artists and of actors of foremost rank, by scenic methods of astonishing simplicity!

It is indeed the first step toward a theatrical renaissance which will rapidly follow if one may accept the verdict of connoisseurs and the enthusiasm of a select audience.

DR. RENÉ PRÉVÔT

Le Figaro (Paris), No. 233:

The Season in Munich—The Artists' Theatre
(By Special Correspondent)

Munich, August 18, 1908

Some of the many evidences of the artistic and gala spirit of Bavaria are most charming. They are worthy of serious discussion and thoughtful criticism, and are too impressive to lend themselves to mere pleasantries. To be sure, this earnest appetite for culture, this measured march toward grace and freedom, cannot yet entirely beguile us, but our curiosity is aroused.

Of these efforts perhaps the most complete is that of the Artists' Theatre. At any rate, it is the most significant. I happened to attend it between a presentation of shadow pictures and a performance of marionettes, both "artistic" and well executed considering the fact that they presented Hans Sachs and Goethe and Maeterlinck one after the other. I expected to find here the spirit that is characteristic of a studio farce or of a sort of cabaret.

I was soon disabused of this idea, and this is what I saw. The rising of the curtain revealed an inner proscenium, a middle stage and an inner stage, sometimes on one level, and sometimes on different levels. At the sides and continually visible are two square towers of wood, each with a door and a window, plain and without colored glass. A movable bridge unites them above, a bridge which carries a complete outfit of lights and which may be raised and lowered at will. Lowered at its farthest point upstage until it almost approaches the curtains, it diminishes considerably the dimensions of the scene and suffices to create of itself the frame of an extremely intimate interior. The second scene is bounded on the right and left sometimes by a movable frame supporting curtains when an interior scene is to be played on the second level, sometimes by two walls when a more open space is desired. These two walls are both movable. They may be completely withdrawn on wagons into the wings, or, on the other hand, they may be brought together so as to shut off the horizon. By means of these walls a street, a church, a prison, the gate to a city, or a château is represented. In the left wall may be distinguished a shallow door and a window. The less important accessories, such as the fountain in *Faust* or the pointed arch in *Twelfth Night*, are enough to transform the character of the scene.

The third level is separated from the back cloth by a chasm, sometimes filled in and sometimes not by a decorative accessary such as a flight of steps or a terraced slope showing the edge of a descending road.

Four back cloths, which a machine unrolls to right and left, constitute the sky for all the scenes.

What principles are embodied in the creation of this theatre and what desires does it satisfy?

The principles have been set forth with great particularity in the works of Georg Fuchs, writer and creator of the Artists' Theatre, by Max Littmann, his architect, and by a number of the foremost architects of Munich, among others by Adolf von Hildebrand.

"Thus far," says Hildebrand, "the association between the plastic arts and the drama has always existed at the expense of the latter. If, for instance, one thought to heighten a play's appeal by a decoration more or less luxurious, one has, on the contrary, diminished if not abolished its appeal." It is, then, to a certain extent, the liberation of the drama which Fuchs attempts, and it is perhaps also the liberation of the poet, enslaved until now not only by the imagination of the painter but also by that of the mechanician.

"The real drama," Hildebrand says again, "should make the spectator live dramatically. What is important in decoration is not the reproduction in all its details of the exact image of the spot where the action occurs but the creation as vivid as possible of the illusion that constitutes drama. The condition of the dramatic life is 'poetic truth' and not 'reality.' Anything added to this hinders the intimate communion between the poet and his public."

The problem then was to find a suitable balance between necessity and superfluity, to create a harmony which satisfies without ever causing us to withdraw from the action for the contemplation of a beautiful vision of plastic art. The reform is not directed solely against the "insolent affluence" of production but also against the tendency of certain artists to decorate the drama "in a fairy-like manner."

"There are spectators like infants," continues Hildebrand; "if you give them a doll too perfectly imitated, their imagination has nothing more to invent; the doll with its coarse realism has spoiled their little world of the imagination, and they do not know what to do with a useless plaything."

This, primarily, is the fundamental thought of the whole system: give the spectators the motive power of suggestion. It was this idea that pervaded the conversations I had with Georg Fuchs and with Benno Becker, one of the directors of the theatre.

Georg Fuchs, before launching his project, set forth the principal features of it in a pamphlet entitled *The Stage of the Future*.

I saw two offerings at the Artists' Theatre—Shakespeare's *Twelfth Night*, and the first part of Goethe's *Faust*. By analyzing some of the scenes of these plays one sees more easily the point which Fuchs is trying to make.

In the Shakespearian play the backdrop represents uniformly a maritime decoration. Fuchs gave me the reason for this uniformity: "The play is concerned," he told me, "with a legend of the sea. It is the sea which determines all the action; the casting away of Sebastian and Viola, and consequently the love of Viola and the Duke of Illyria. It is the sea, therefore, which should preside over the development of the plot."

The arrival of Sebastian and of Viola has as a setting the entrance to the town. The two walls of which I spoke above are drawn together, an arch joins them in the middle. In the distance one sees the ocean, and below in the third plane a sail. The second plane is raised and is joined to the first by a flight of steps. The two towers (the bridge between them having been raised to the flies) give the suggestion of two houses, and the illusion of the entrance to a maritime city is complete.

The scene in which Sir Toby, Sir Andrew, and the fool become intoxicated is similarly arranged. The two walls somewhat drawn together suggest an arch which looks out on a dimly illuminated sky. The second plane, which is elevated, is set with a long table and two benches. The two towers seem to be a part of a large hall in a great castle. A diffused light envelops the characters, and once again the impression is complete.

There is not a single scene in the Shakespearian play in which the modesty of the staging detracts from the poetry of the performance. Quite the contrary. I would not say the same of *Faust*. The Walpurgis scene and that in the witches' kitchen seem to me to have fallen short in effectiveness. They are, moreover, the only scenes which deviate slightly from the system and in which the illusion is destroyed by an attempt at a more complicated realism. With these exceptions, the play takes on a highly artistic character. The theatre in Weimar, with a budget of a hundred thousand marks, never succeeded in producing one of Goethe's masterpieces without loading it down with a heavy and tasteless scene. Here, by simple means, the play preserves all its atmosphere and all its poetry.

The prologue alone would justify the claims of Georg Fuchs. It is not exactly easy to represent Heaven! Teeming clouds, chubby angels in pink tights playing trumpets, a venerable god, half Neptune, half St. Nicholas—these are the things that are usually shown us. Here there is nothing of that. The backdrop is pure white and strongly lighted. The third plane is raised and serves as a sort of high relief against which three archangels stand out. The roles of the angels are taken by actors of heroic size who, standing on little platforms which are disguised by folds of yellow material flowing from their waists, seem still more imposing. Their arms are bare, their breasts are covered by heavy bronze armor, their heads are motionless, their eyes fixed. St. Michael, St. Raphael, and St. Gabriel carry horizontally gigantic swords and are supported by huge brazen pinions the tips of which seem to sink to the bottom of the space which divides the scene from the backcloth. All this is simple but powerful in effect. I cannot imagine that the usual childish procedures could ever produce so overwhelming an impression.

The scene in the garden is charming. The walls have disappeared and have been replaced by trellises of green wood over which climb plants and flowers. A bench on the right, moonlight, and the impression is exquisite.

For the cathedral scene the wall on the left represents a large pillar at the foot of which leans Marguerite. The crowd turns its back on the public and is lost in the obscurity of the second and third planes. Upstage one chandelier in which some church candles burn feebly mysteriously illuminates the shadows. And this is much more magnificent than the most lofty arches or the most imposing nave.

There remains only the question of the costumes and the lighting. The former is left entirely to the imagination of the artist. For *Faust,* which is so "established," the experiment is more dangerous than for Shakespeare. It seemed to me, nevertheless, conclusive. If the sight of a designedly brunette Marguerite was somewhat surprising, the really superior talent of an artist like Lina Lossen and the beauty of the poetry were amply sufficient to concentrate the attention on essentials. As for the rest, if the appearance of the peasants, the citizens, and the harvesters astonished us, let us admit that it was not our profound knowledge of historic costume that made us so critical but rather the flouting of sanctified but fallacious tradition.

Light is the principal factor in the presentations of the Artists' Theatre. It is light that liberates the imagination.

Not the footlights, which are extremely reduced. A circular opening situated in the proscenium floor occasionally supplies a feeble light, which is then reflected on a metal strip, a light scarcely noticeable, which gives a faint color to the ground. The actors are always illuminated from above and from the depths. They are always represented in *relief*. This is one of the happiest innovations of the new theatre. The scene between Faust and his familiar spirit is, from this point of view, one of supreme beauty. The two black silhouettes stand out strikingly against a background of hills plunged in the darkness of night. The dialogue unfolds and the history of the water spaniel, almost always comic, now acquires an unprecedented vigor and a fantastic quality heretofore unequaled.

The artists of the Artists' Theatre do not use much make-up; and the impression they make is no less intense.

Finally, the acting seems to be freer than on the ordinary stage. Unencumbered by a multiplicity of effects and accessories, the actors seem to pay a more sustained attention to the text and to interpret it more faithfully and movingly.

What will be the significance of the Artists' Theatre? The future will decide this important question. Whatever may come of it, the Artists' Theatre deserves the attention of all those who are interested in dramatic art.

Moreover, it is not solely the idea that should be applauded but the immediate and spontaneous success that it has achieved from the very beginning, the response that this artistic experiment—artistic in the best sense of the word—has met with in official circles.

Here is an undertaking of the most audacious sort which runs counter to all the ideas of the traditional theatre. Do you know who is its foremost patron? Prince Rupprecht of Bavaria. Who is the musical director? Felix Mottl, the director of the local opera. Who is its greatest admirer? Herr von Speidel himself, the superintendent of the royal theatres who loans to it his own artists. And all this has been done simply, without any excitement, without insurmountable obstacles. And this is perhaps more worth consideration than all the rest.

ROBERT BRUSSEL

Kölnische Volkszeitung (Cologne), June 14, 1908:

For years we have been hearing of the need for reform in the theatre. People are tired of painted realism which, with its overelaborate and grandiose pretentions, merely calls attention to its expensive artificiality. Away with wings and borders, with footlights and the stage of too great depth! The auditorium should be built as an amphitheatre around the playing space, and on the stage pictures should be shown, pictures that stand out boldly in relief and merely serve to frame the dramatic action.

Thus our theatre would abandon the style derived more than two hundred years ago from the royal courts of the Renaissance and would approach the ideal to which Goethe, Schinkel, and Semper aspired. The Englishman, Gordon Craig, advocates a middle ground between the old stage arrangements and the newest reform. In his opinion, action, speech, line, and color should be unified, under the direction of the *régisseur*, so as to appeal most of all to the eye. The spoken word is for him only *one* element in the synthesis of agencies employed in presenting a poetic work upon the stage. The effort made at Munich to bring out the dramatic content by means of the spoken word, seems to me to be more correct. In this way the art of acting achieves more freshness and validity.

The first performance at which the theories of the Artists' Theatre could be clearly presented and evaluated was that of *Faust*. The achievement was overwhelming and unforgettable. Although here and there further improvements might be suggested, the venture must be accounted successful and indicative of future developments even in respect to its smallest details. . . . We believe that we can best communicate to the reader the true spirit of the performance if we describe it, scene by scene.

The whole stage space has a depth of only eight meters; for this particular play scarcely half of it was used. The separate scenes must be imagined as action unfolding like a frieze in relief.

Prologue in Heaven—The three archangels, youthful male figures of heroic size with pinions of brass like the outward-opening wings of a mighty bronze gate, stand on the narrow steps of a lofty elevation. Enveloping their breasts and arms are sheets of mail, and horizontally in their hands they hold mighty swords. They emanate a monumental and awesome power. In the background a pale yellow canvas flooded with light stretches away into infinity. In the foreground one sees Mephisto crouching, clad in the brownish habit of a scholar. Music sounds, awakening in us the expectation of an approaching presence. With increasing clarity and power resounds the angels' song and the music of the spheres. The voice of God reaches us from infinite space. Lifting his head to the endless distances of Heaven, Mephisto speaks. A roar of wind—and night devours the spirit of darkness.

Faust's Study—In a bare and massive wall one sees a niche before which hangs a curtain. On the left a small door; above it a shelf of books. On the right a fireplace. Downstage left a narrow window; on the right an exit. An armchair stands before a heavy desk. The space is feebly lighted by a lamp—The space! This is the new element, this feeling of a shut-in world that is inspired and sustained with little artifice in matters of perspective. Here, as in the following scenes, everything unimportant is eliminated. We see only what is necessary for us to see to understand the situation. With the appearance of the Earth Spirit, whose voice alone we hear, the walls take on color as though blood ran from their pores; the curtain changes to the deep blue of the ocean's surface; Faust's silhouette stands out against it in dark purple. In plastic relief, without the old stupidities, we are shown the struggle of a soul in solitary torment.

The Easter Parade—Once more there is a great canvas, which appears to be an expanse of orange-tinted sky, with below, a chain of gently undulating hills in early spring colors. In front is a platform about forty centimeters wide, from which one looks down upon the landscape as from a high wall. Here, and on the road which lies somewhat lower, the pleasure-seeking promenaders wander up and down. They are of varied types. A large number is unnecessary. Finally Faust appears: worn, sorrowful, yet with the free bearing of one who is revived, like a convalescent. Behind him in black garments, vulgar, complacent, and officious, comes Wagner. Now the stream of people is more plentiful; finally there is music and dancing—a really brilliant scene, which is delicately played in the smallest space. One gets the feeling of a festival, with all its crowds and many-colored life, and yet one sees few more than a dozen people. By means of a clever disposition of space and by the arrangement of the individual actors, the illusion of spontaneity is created. The picture lives, without being a "living picture"; its colors and rhythms do not exist independently but are reflections of the poetic content.

Now slowly evening approaches. Faust and Wagner are alone on the stage. In their outward appearance they are sharply contrasted; they do not need to exchange a word. The twilight deepens to an almost emerald light in which their two deep-violet figures move as at the bottom of the sea. The ghostly hound is invisible. He lies in a corner and this fact increases the overpowering horror of the impression until the climax is reached with the sudden appearance of Mephisto as a scholar in crimson robes.

Auerbach's Cellar—This is almost the same scene as Faust's study. Where the curtain was before there is now a recessed wall. Where the fireplace was is a table with a pair of benches. Steps lead down on the left, and toward the foreground stands a cask. Here again is the distinct feeling of an underground vaulted cellar with its coolness and seclusion.

The Witches' Kitchen—Here the usual artificial atmosphere of romantic brigandry is absent. A single broken wall creates a sort of cavern, where a phosphorescent darkness rules. In front of the window-opening stands a mighty bubbling kettle, busily stirred by two monkeylike cats about the size of twelve-year-old children. On the left wall is a frame, in which later in misty garments the floating form of Helena may be vaguely seen. The part of the witch, clad in a plain, blue-gray garment, with two scant pigtails on her balding head, was taken by a man. In this way the wild character of this unlovely being was emphasized. Faust and Mephisto stand out sharply in this scene, which is hampered by no other decorations.

The Entrance to the Church—In the background are the projecting façades of two towerlike buildings. Between them in the middle appears a sort of window. Here Gretchen wanders by. One has the impression of a narrow street in which the girl cannot escape Faust's approach, and the constraint and oppressiveness of the situation is thus vitally strengthened.

Gretchen's Room (An Idyll)—This is approximately the actual size of a young girl's modest chamber. In the middle of the wall is a window about a meter in width and correspondingly high with leaded panes and wreathed with flowers; in an angle of the wall an armchair and opposite it a table. At the left in front of the entrance is a linen curtain and next to it a cupboard; on the right a little niche for the bed—everything very clean and simple but not impoverished. Everything has a poetic quality of virginal enchantment. Now Gretchen appears in immaculate gray-blue garments! A fairy picture by Schwind she seems, or at least a reminder of his early studies. Then, as the blue shadows of evening gather and Gretchen, heavyhearted, sits in her chair, one is oppressed by the sense of impending sorrow as through parting painfully from the peaceful, childish happiness of youth.

Martha's Chamber—This is exactly the opposite of Gretchen's room. In front of a large window there hangs as a curtain a sort of counterpane, elaborate but tasteless. To the left and right of this is only the bare wall with its one door. A somber, cheerless interior which emphasizes sharply the contrast between the two shown in the conversation that follows.

The Arbor—Here is a green lattice with climbing roses, centered beyond a portal; on the right a bench. A step behind this so that we have the effect of a passage is a wall; on the edge of this in green boxes luxuriant geraniums. So Faust and Gretchen, Mephisto and Martha, may promenade separately. Every single figure stands out like a high relief from its surroundings, but it is given such life by the flood of evening sunshine, by the twilight that follows, and by the veil of moonlight that we see before us real people of flesh and blood—but transfigured by the poetic atmosphere. At the second meeting of Faust and Gretchen this scene has the effect of a picture by Erler that has come alive. The colors have all the soft opalescent gleam of mother-of-pearl.

Faust in the Mountains—A yellow moon hangs in a night-blue sky, and its rays form a pyramid above towering snow-capped mountains which fall away precipitately; in the foreground brown, black and bluish rocks. The whole thing once more is only a painted canvas with a few set pieces and yet creates a solitude which almost swallows up mere man. Out of it Faust speaks into the still infinity. The figure of Mephisto enters like a threatening, strangely smoldering torch.

Gretchen at the Spinning Wheel—One is reminded of Velásquez's world-famous *Tapestry Workers*. In front of a great, dark curtain sits Gretchen and turns her spinning wheel. From above on the left the moonlight falls through a narrow opening and makes a swaying, shimmering light along the curtain, across the eddying movement of Gretchen's dress with its threads of gold. The tremulous movement of light symbolizes Gretchen's longing, and her agitation is like the fluttering of a bird in a narrow cage.

At the Well—Again there is only the long, unadorned façade of a row of houses, in a niche of which is the well—quite similar in its simplicity to the scene for Valentine's death. Here was an opportunity to design pictures with particular consideration for color and movement. They were completely successful. Here lavender, yellow, and dark brown prevailed, there gray, white, blue, red, green, and black were combined in a choice harmony, the tones of which were probably softened by the moonlight. We were not shown people in knots and crowds but again in a sort of relief effect that seemed to be artistically balanced in itself.

In the Church—The scene represents the entrance to a basilica. The people rise like pale frescoes out of the darkness. Gretchen leans against a pillar. From above a sharp voice hurls its accusing phrases like dagger thrusts into the convulsive soul of the maiden, who cringes in quiet helplessness. Suddenly a trumpet sounds, and the choral chant of the *Deis irae* is heard. The whole church is not shown. We perceive a stretch of blackness rather than the mysterious darkness of an old-fashioned house of God. Nevertheless, the scene is deeply moving precisely because of its unadorned simplicity.

Walpurgis Night—Before a vast sky, which is faintly illuminated, rises the sharp outline of a mountain height. On the left a pine, on the right the giant gravestone. Laboriously, Faust and Mephisto climb the inner slope. Scarcely have they arrived at the summit when fiery steam surrounds them as from the bowels of the earth. The black silhouettes of ghosts and witches come nearer and nearer, their number increasing, their movements becoming wilder and more abandoned until all are entangled in a bewildering maze. Then Gretchen appears, walking slowly with fettered feet. With one stroke everything is plunged in darkness. It was really only a wild and ghostly dream. The mood of this scene might be heightened. At present there is too much shadow play and too little plastic form. For that a more forceful design would be necessary.

The Dungeon Scene—Here is a long wall, in the middle a barred door. Steps descend on the left—the entrance to the inescapable depths. An awesome effect is achieved without the help of intricate artifices. One feels that here is where the last act must take place.

Thus it is that the intellectual abundance of *Faust,* its dramatic power as well as its delicate lyric quality, comes to complete and living expression through the expedients which we have so briefly described. The actor too achieves a newer, higher, and more complete significance in his speech, his action, and his pictorial quality; he must, to be sure, subordinate himself more than formerly to the whole, but he wins from the resulting harmony a heightening of his own performance.

How long will it be before such productions, which, although not perfect, still give promise of perfection, will be imitated on our leading stages? Only then will it be possible to raise the theatre to the heights of art and to the level of a spiritual experience.

Dr. Jos. Popp

Münchener Post (Munich), June 9, 1908:

First Goethe, now Shakespeare! Once more a great work as a test of the new art of design. And once more the great work has not been put to shame on the little picture stage, nor has the little picture stage been put to shame by the great work. Many managers and *régisseurs* have tried their hand at Shakespeare's gaily colored carnival piece *Twelfth Night*, and we believe that the wearisome Meiningen school came closest to perfection. I still remember very well their ponderous theatrical apparatus.

It was easy to predict that Julius Diez was the man to transform the scene into color so that all would be marvelous harmony. For in his art he has the happy combination of fertile imagination and ingenious practicality, of fabulous and palpable conceptions such as are demanded by the spirit of Shakespeare's piece. And so, for the first time, we see Shakespeare's *Twelfth Night* realized in pictures of radiant beauty; we see for the first time also the flow of life, the wealth of wit, the brilliance and abandon of the separate scenes harmoniously and artistically blended.

Allgemeine Zeitung (Munich), June 18 1908:

The performance of *Twelfth Night* staged by Julius Diez showed in an exemplary manner just what the Artists' Theatre can do. The whole thing was an artistic unity in the finest style and the work of the painter was indissolubly mingled with that of the *régisseur*. The most beautiful and artistic pictures coincided exactly with the best scenes of of the performance. The individual figures stood out in a wonderfully plastic manner, and one thing in particular was typical: the whole procession of pictures appeared colorful, indeed sumptuous, in spite of the simplification and stylization of the scene. There was no puritanical restraint to annoy. There was, indeed, as much illusion as if offered by the richest of naturalistic productions of the previous theatrical style.

FRITZ FREIHERR VON OSTINI

Allgemeine Zeitung (Munich), August 8, 1908:

We have had to wait some time for the last bill at the Artists' Theatre. Certain skeptical persons even doubted whether they would get to see it at all. Day before yesterday, however, the promise was fulfilled, and fulfilled, moreover, with the happiest results. There was this time in the audience no high-strung, anxious reservations concerning critical opinion. Well-being and merriment seemed to be both general and inescapable in the packed house.

The hilarious comedy of Krähwinkel about the theatrical king of the Biedermeier period was given especially, according to the notice on the program, because the producers wished to show "that even a conventional conversation piece which has no literary quality but which in everyday theatrical experience is by far the most popular," may achieve a completely artistic effect, if the scenic design is artistic and *régisseur* and performer are genuinely creative artists. Whether the decisive and, to all appearances, very encouraging result, which day before yesterday's presentation of *Deutsche Kleinstädter* achieved according to the new manner of stage setting, has proved that this new manner is the most ideally artistic and practically efficient method of production for *every sort* of conventional play of dialogue, I must make bold to doubt. But it has shown quite clearly that such a play of middle-class bourgeois society, in so far as it also demands no depth of stage, loses nothing in the new stage frame, provided it has artistic mounting, careful direction, and good acting. It is indeed more likely to gain in intimate atmospheric effect by the valuable co-operation of plastic art and particularly by the advantages which a more controllable illumination affords. Even the much-debated stationary "towers" proved their incontrovertible value. No damage was done to the mood of the play because the hopeful Sperling, Substitute Inspector of Buildings and Roads, intoned his mighty love song from the eminence of one of these towers. The achievements of Thomas Theodor Heine in the scenic decoration of the piece deserve unbounded recognition, even from the standpoint of the dramatic action. The room that he created in the burgomaster's house offered a frame for the first acts which was as artistic and charming as it was harmonious with the character of the action. The glimmering twilight of the street scene in the final act fitted no less harmoniously into the atmosphere of the whole drama. In the treatment of masks and costumes Heine was also quite free from all picturesque extravagances. Only when the play itself called for them did he use the grotesque peculiarities of the epoch with strong effect.

Basil took charge of the direction. His great care in the training of a lively and humorous yet finely detailed acting ensemble also deserves the highest praise. The complete satisfaction with which the performance was received found expression in storms of applause at the close of the acts, and still more in the convincing heartiness of the laughter.

HANNS VON GUMPPENBERG

[N.p., n.d.]

In his work as a painter, as an illustrator of *Simplicissimus*, and as a most tasteful designer of furniture, Thomas Theodor Heine has always shown such a candid preference for the Biedermeier style that one could probably not find a more able worker to outfit a play according to the taste of that period. Not only does Heine know the characteristic forms of the Biedermeier style as few others know them, but he is completely at home in the spirit of the period, in its comfort that is yet a trifle stiff and cool, in its sprawling elegance and droll grandiloquence. And so it was certain from the beginning that Heine's production of *Deutsche Kleinstädter* would offer us scenic pictures that were authentic in style and charming in humor. The play itself suited the taste of the artist in every particular, and one felt that all these provincial figures were only waiting for Heine to costume them. It obviously did not suffice him to have the costumes "genuine." He characterized each individual accurately by means of his costumes and enlivened the whole play by a great number of delicately comic nuances. A treatment of color that was both clever and consciously artistic contributed to bring this about. The way in which the different couples in the play were effectively contrasted—for instance, "he and she," the serious and the comic lover, the two aunts—the way in which, in the red and gold room during the first three acts, all shades of red became gradually intensified—in the dress of the housemaids, in the costume of one of the aunts, in the coat of the lover, and so on—all these things showed a great cultivation and sureness of taste. If the Munich Artists' Theatre had done nothing more than to point out to stage directors and *régisseurs* the paramount importance of color in the stage picture it would be sufficient achievement.

Heine furnished the room in the first act with genuine old cherry furniture, and the effect was as genuine as could be although he remained true to the principle of the stage and worked without sidewalls or ceiling and with only a modified perspective (*prospekt*). This time Heine gave more details than would be called for by a merely suggestive and symbolic production. Genuine vases, lamps, bowls, and boxes stood about, genuine old portraits, engravings, and rows of silhouettes hung on the wall, and there was a great deal of furniture, and so forth. The decoration of the room was accomplished within the technique of the reform stage, but the result was absolutely realistic. And whenever one wishes to represent modern interiors on these boards, one will always have to work with these means. The more the literary characteristics of the drama bring out subtle touches, the more intimacy the stage itself demands. For the pithy style of Shakespeare the indication of the locality in a general way is quite sufficient. And so in each case the scene must be handled differently. A reform that merely substituted new patterns for the old ones would not be worth lifting a finger for.

The decoration of the final act shows, lying in the moonlight, the little old town of Krähwinkel, which has become famous because of this piece—a prospect as beautiful and delicately atmospheric as has ever been seen. In this splendidly successful scene the appearance of great distance was attained, although the space from the proscenium to the back wall was only a few feet deep. This signifies a triumph for the technical apparatus as well as for the artist who was so clever in understanding its use.

F. v. O.

Translator's Notes

Translator's Preface

1. Among the most important of these are:

Huntly Carter, *The New Spirit in Drama and Art* (New York: Mitchell Kennerly, 1913).

Sheldon Cheney, *The Art Theatre* (New York: Alfred A. Knopf, 1925).

——, *The New Movement in the Theatre* (New York: Mitchell Kennerly, 1914).

——, *Stage Decoration* (New York: The John Day Co., 1928).

——, *The Theatre: Three Thousand Years of Drama, Acting, and Stagecraft* (New York: Tudor Publishing Co., 1935).

Thomas H. Dickinson, *The Theatre in a Changing Europe* (New York: Henry Holt and Co., 1937).

Mordecai Gorelik, *New Theatres for Old* (New York: Samuel French, 1952).

Glenn Hughes, *The Story of the Theatre* (New York: Samuel French, 1928).

Theodore Kornisarjevsky, *The Theatre in a Changing Civilization* (London, 1935).

Kenneth Macgowan, *The Theatre of Tomorrow* (New York: Boni and Liveright, 1921).

Hiram Kelly Moderwell, *The Theatre of Today* (New York: Dodd, Mead and Co., 1925).

Thomas Wood Stevens, *The Theatre from Athens to Broadway* (New York: D. Appleton and Co., 1932).

2. *Manfred: Tragödie in 4 Aufzügen* (Darmstadt: A. Berg-Strasser, 1903); *Don Quichote: Der sinnreiche Junker von Mancha, musikalische Tragikomödie in 3 Aufzügen nach Miguel de Cervantes Saavedra*, Musik von Anton Beer-Walbrunn (Munich: G. Mueller, 1907).

3. *Von der stilistischen Belebung der Schaubühne* (Leipzig: E. Diedrichs, 1891); *Die Schaubühne der Zukunft* (Berlin and Leipzig: Shuster u. Loeffler, 1905).

4. *Wir Zuchthäusler. Erinnerungen des Zellengefangener nr. 2911, im Zuchthause geschrieben* (Munich: A. Langen, 1931).

I. The Theatre and Culture

1. European playgoers have been accustomed to approach the theatre in a different spirit from that which animates American audiences. This was particularly true in the period preceding World War I, when a more leisurely way of life existed for that class of society which, in general, supported the theatre.

Most of the German theatres at this time were repertory companies, which offered several different plays in the course of a week. No definite curtain time could be taken for granted by the audience, because each production was scheduled to begin at the hour deemed most suitable for that particular play. Attendance at a theatre was a social event for which the European playgoer was accustomed to make arrangements in advance. To be tardy at a performance was considered unmannerly, and in certain instances latecomers were refused admission to the auditorium during the course of an act.

Continental theatres were built with large foyers with adequate wardrobe space where members of the audience were expected to check their wraps. To have entered the auditorium in one's coat and hat would have been both awkward and unnecessary. Evening dress, while not mandatory, was usual, and the audience was accustomed to be conscious of itself as well as of the play.

Intermissions in Continental theatres were longer than in America, and large lounges, promenades, buffets, and restaurant facilities furnished an environment hospitable to a leisurely and relaxed enjoyment of theatregoing as a social experience.

Moreover, the Munich Artists' Theatre represented the festival idea, which was familiar to European audiences. The Exposition Park which surrounded it was an important adjunct, just as the beauty of the Bavarian Alps and the charm of the village of Oberammergau contributed to the effect of the Passion Play and the picturesque scenery of Salzburg added luster to the dramatic productions of Max Reinhardt.

2. The author reflects the temper of a time when Germany had been at peace for forty years, when even the Imperial military pomp had become a stereotype. The susceptibility of the German public to the emotional excitement of pageantry as it was later exploited by Hitler has been frequently discussed. For a description of Nazi festivals see Edgar Ansel Mowrer, *Germany Puts the Clock Back* (New York: Morrow, 1939), "A Showman of Genius."

3. Fuchs began his studies of the theatre at the time when "closet drama," as exemplified by the Browning cult in England, was in high favor among the literati.

4. This device of announcing the rise of the curtain by a musical chime of bells was a feature of the productions of David Belasco. Although the romanticized naturalism of Belasco's productions was far removed from the simplification and stylization of the Munich Artists' Theatre, his interest in the creation of a receptive mood in the audience was similar.

5. For illustrations of such theatres see *The Stage Yearbook for 1912*, edited by L. Carson. Photographs of the municipal theatres at Dortmund and Lübeck designed by the architect Martin Dülfer of Dresden illustrate the type of building to which Fuchs refers. The same volume contains a sketch by Max Littmann of his design for the Court Theatre at Stuttgart, which

in contrast to the illustrations just mentioned immediately shows its superiority.

6. For a description of the theatre as a tribunal see Mordecai Gorelik, *New Theatres for Old.* The Munich Artists' Theatre was founded on the assumption that the climate of any theatre is more conducive to emotion than to cerebration: that an individual is unlikely to do his most valid thinking in the company of several hundred other people and that the intellectual concepts of a play should be analyzed before the performance by those who produce it and afterwards by those who witness it.

7. For Ostini's criticism of one of the performances at the Munich Artists' Theatre see Appendix, pp. 198, 202.

III. The Actor

1. Exhibitions of hypnotism were of general interest during the latter part of the nineteenth century. The success of George du Maurier's popular novel, *Trilby,* was an evidence of this interest. The dancer described by Fuchs was the subject of a detailed study concerning the psychological bases of dramatic art: Dr. Freiherr von Schrenk-Notzing, Prakt. Artzt in München, *Die Traumtänzerin, Madeleine G.: Eine Psychologische Studie Über Hypnose und Dramatische Kunst* (Stuttgart: Verlag von Ferdinand Enke, 1904).

IV. Stage and Auditorium

1. The achievements of the Artists' Theatre have, in the past half-century, become so thoroughly incorporated into the techniques of modern stagecraft that it is now difficult to appreciate the magnitude of their significance at the time of their inception. In the light of the present, however, the most significant thing about *Die Revolution des Theaters* is that it is the history of a *successful professional enterprise.* For, while educational and nonprofessional dramatic organizations have increased in number for the past three decades, the number of first class professional enterprises has steadily declined.

2. This does not describe a general practice of the period but refers specifically to the type of staging used at the Redoutensaal

in Vienna. For a description of these productions see Kenneth Macgowan and Robert Edmond Jones, *Continental Stagecraft* (New York: Harcourt, Brace and Co., 1922), ch. iv.

VI. Opera

1. During the past half-century new techniques in the staging of opera have derived mainly from two sources: first, from Appia, who by his experimentation in the staging of Wagner's *Gesamtkunstwerke* (syntheses of art forms) developed the theory that every element of a production—the lighting, the color, the scenery, the costumes, and the movement—is established by the music; and second, from the experimentations in acting techniques, such as those of Stanislavsky, which have been applied to the improvement of acting in opera as well as in drama. Opera singers today recognize the necessity for disciplines which make them visually as well as musically convincing. Thus, the best of such performers have come to accept obligations toward their audiences that are similar to those which Fuchs desired to impose upon all actors in dramatic productions.

VII. Vaudeville

1. The admiration which, during the late nineteenth and early twentieth century, artists in Munich evinced for the achievements of music-hall performers parallels the appreciation shown during the same period by outstanding artists in Paris. Degas, Gauguin, and Toulouse-Lautrec used vaudeville performers, as models for some of their most notable pictures.

VIII. The History of the Artists' Theatre

1. "Gottfried Semper expresses himself in detail on this subject in an article appearing in 1849 about the so-called 'old theatre' in Dresden, in which he discusses an early plan, first made in 1835, but never carried out. This plan contained all the ideas about stage arrangement with which we are concerned today. He narrowed the stage very decidedly and says in this connection:

'In the first place, a truly artistic effect in stage decoration is made easier because the shifting of cumbersome wings is made superfluous, and a single very broad background, the edges of which are hidden by the walls of the proscenium (which are not far apart) can supply the essential elements of decoration by a painted panorama. Because the proscenium opening is far back, it furnishes a frame for the stage picture, which is a very desirable thing from an artistic point of view and, in the eyes of a cultivated audience, makes the playing space more vivid. Moreover, the stage can be effectively lighted, which under ordinary circumstances is generally impossible. The actor wants to be flooded with light. If he is in the midst of the scenery, then it too must of necessity be brightly lighted also. But stage decoration needs an entirely different sort of illumination in order to be effective, and therefore it should be separated in space from the playing area.

'Secondly, such an arrangement of the stage is optically and acoustically advantageous and gives the impression that the action has, so to speak, moved into the very center of the auditorium.

'The third advantage is the most important. The prevailing bad practice of having parades and processions march down from the farthest possible point upstage and thus give a slap in the face to all sense of perspective or good taste, will be impossible. It is easy to see that smaller mass movements are much more effective. At any rate, their ineffectiveness is more easily disguised and their ridiculous aspects avoided if such processions are shown us in profile, as is allowed, or even necessitated, by this stage arrangement. On the whole, one can only wish that the current striving after pictorial or picturesque groupings might give way to the classic principles, far more favorable to dramatic art, of plastic, or rather, relief-like arrangement of figures' " (Max Littmann, *Das Münchner Künstlertheater* [Munich: L. Werner, 1908], p. 11).

2. Wagner had found the Court Theatre in Munich a difficult place in which to work. He was unable to co-operate with the theatre management and resented having to fit his productions into the over-all schedule for the theatre season. In his

desire not only to please Wagner but also to put an end to the intrigues and controversies which were harassing the theatre intendant, King Ludwig commissioned the architect Gottfried Semper to draw plans for a festival theatre in Munich which was to house Wagner's music dramas exclusively.

"We [Cosima, Bülow, and myself] saw the model," Wagner wrote to Ludwig on the second of January, 1867, "and we are unanimously of the opinion that if this building is constructed there will be nothing of its kind in modern Europe to be compared with it. It is a marvel: my idea, my instructions, my requirements have been completely comprehended by Semper's genius" (Ernest Newman, *The Life of Richard Wagner* [New York: Alfred A. Knopf, 1946], IV, 296, note).

Semper's plans were never carried out. The project for a festival house in Munich was abandoned in favor of the Bayreuth project and the festival house in Bayreuth was put in the hands of other architects.

IX. The New Art of the Stage and the Commercial Theatre

1. Fuchs' pride in the fact that the Artists' Theatre was established on a sound financial basis is worthy of note. The designation commercial as applied to the professional theatre should not in itself be considered a term of opprobrium.

Acknowledgments

I SHOULD like to express my thanks to the members of the Drummond Bequest Committee of Cornell University for their careful consideration of my manuscript and to Carolyn Cooley, who as head of the Drummond Fund gave constant support and encouragement. I am deeply indebted to Frances Eagan of the School of Industrial and Labor Relations at Cornell, whose generous and knowledgeable contribution of time and attention made possible the first version of the manuscript. To Mary Virginia Heinlein, director of the Vassar Experimental Theatre, I am grateful for her kindness in reading part of the manuscript, and I should like to acknowledge the helpful interest shown by Barnard Hewitt, of the University of Illinois, representing the American Educational Theatre Association. And most particularly I am grateful to my husband, Theodore Kuhn, for his assistance with every aspect of the preparation of the book.

Index

Index

Index

Index

Index

Index

Index